Contents

Preface

Is civil society the 'big idea' for the twenty-first century, or will the idea of civil society – confused, corrupted or captured by elites – prove another false horizon in the search for a better world? By illuminating the uses and abuses of different civil society theories, I hope this book will help readers of different persuasions to answer this question for themselves.

Civil society has become a notoriously slippery concept, used to justify radically different ideological agendas, supported by deeply ambiguous evidence, and suffused with many questionable assumptions. Faced by these ambiguities, it is tempting to dismiss this concept as hopelessly compromised, but I will argue the opposite case: when subjected to a rigorous critique, the idea of civil society re-emerges to offer significant emancipatory potential, explanatory power, and practical support to problem solving in both established and emerging democracies. However, this positive conclusion holds only when we abandon the search for theoretical consensus and embrace the fact that civil society does indeed mean different things to different people, plays different roles at different times, and constitutes both problem and solution. What is important about the civil society debate is not that one school of thought is proved correct and others exposed as false, but the extent to which different frameworks can generate insights that lead to more effective action. Recognizing that civil society is contested territory – in both theory and reality – is the first step in rescuing a potentially powerful set of ideas from the conceptual confusion that threatens to submerge them.

My aim in this book is to encourage readers to come to a more informed and nuanced set of judgements about the civil society debate, and the first steps in that process are to clarify the origins of different contemporary understandings of this concept and explain why one in particular has risen in popularity so quickly since the fall of the Berlin Wall. These questions are covered in chapter 1, which concludes by highlighting some of the exaggerated claims that have created a backlash against the idea of civil society, and the specific deficiencies of civil society organizations, in academia, journalism, labour unions and government. This backlash may provide a useful corrective in the civil society debate, but taken too far, it threatens to 'throw the baby out with the bath water' to the detriment of progressive social goals and the lives of millions of people across the globe for whom civil society provides a compelling vision in their struggles for a better world. The stakes are very high.

The next step in the argument is to clarify what civil society means in different traditions – there being no interpretation that commands universal assent. The next three chapters explore three different theoretical positions, each useful and legitimate but also incomplete: analytical models of civil society (the forms of associational life, in chapter 2); normative models of civil society (the kind of society they are supposed to generate, in chapter 3); and civil society as the 'public sphere' in chapter 4. The first of these models see civil society as a *part* of society distinct from states and markets, formed for the purposes of advancing common interests and facilitating collective action. Most commonly referred to as the 'third sector', civil society in this sense contains all associations and networks between the family and the state, except firms. However, there is no assumption that these diverse forms of associational life share a normative consensus or a common political agenda – a crucial point in relation to the argument that follows.

The second set of theories define civil society in normative terms – as the realm of service rather than self-interest, and a breeding ground for the 'habits of the heart' – attitudes and values like cooperation, trust, tolerance and non-violence. In this sense, civil society means a *type* of society that is motivated by a different way of being and living in the world, or a different rationality, identified as 'civil'. Although it is often conflated with the first set of theories in circular arguments about 'forms and norms', this model must be seen as separate, for two, interrelated, reasons: first, associations have different normative agendas, and second, the same normative agendas are shaped by different sets of institutions – government and the market as well as voluntary associations.

My third school of thought sees civil society as an arena for public deliberation, rational dialogue and the exercise of 'active citizenship' in pursuit of the common interest – in other words, as the 'public sphere'. Though often ignored in the policy and practice of governments, international agencies and even parts of academia, no understanding of civil society can be complete without a full appreciation of the role played by the public sphere in democracy and development.

Having clarified the differences between these three models of civil society, are we forced to choose between them, or can they be seen as complementary? Chapter 5 argues that elements from each can be combined together into a mutually supportive framework that strengthens the utility of civil society both as an idea and a framework for action. How does a 'strong civil society' in the analytical sense lead to a 'society that is strong and civil' in the normative sense, and what role is played by the public sphere in promoting both? This is the single most important question in the civil society debate, and also the most neglected. Chapter 5 sheds new light on these questions by showing that civil society is simultaneously a goal to aim for, a means to achieve it and a framework for engaging with each other about ends and means.

Finally, what does an integrated approach like this have to say about public policy and the practice of citizen action? The book concludes that there are no solutions to social, economic and political problems in the twenty-first century that do not involve civil society in one or more of its three disguises, and chapter 6 lays out an agenda for nurturing the connections between them that ranges far beyond the anaemic shopping list of community service, non-governmental organization (NGO) capacity building, and a return to some imaginary past that dominates the current civil society discourse in the USA and elsewhere. These orthodox suggestions ignore the structural factors that undermine the health of civil society in each of its manifestations. Much deeper action is required in politics, economics and social life if civil society is to be an effective vehicle for change.

To qualify as a 'big idea' in the century to come, civil society must be able to be described and understood in terms accessible to the sceptic, tested rigorously and successfully against the available empirical evidence, and converted into practical measures that can be deployed in real-world contexts. Thankfully, none of these criteria requires that we accept a single, universal interpretation of civil society in every circumstance, but all of them demand a level of openness and objectivity that has been lacking in much of the discussion to date. I hope that this book, and others, will help to redress that balance.

Acknowledgements

My first thanks go to my colleagues in the Ford Foundation's Governance and Civil Society Program, especially Barry Gaberman, Irena Gross, Christopher Harris, Lisa Jordan, Bradford Smith and Urvashi Vaid, all in New York, and many other colleagues overseas. They provided many helpful ideas and insights, as did non-Ford Foundation friends like John Keane and David Held. I received excellent support from the editorial team at Polity, especially Rachel Kerr. Of course, nothing in this book should be taken as the policy or position of the Ford Foundation.

The first three chapters of the book were written at my parents' home in the English Lake District, and my thanks go to them for surrendering their precious privacy during the Christmas of 2002 and the new year of 2003. The rest of the book was written in upstate New York, where my wife Cora sacrificed many weekends together so that I could complete the book more or less on schedule. As my own 'civil society', this book is dedicated to her.

Michael Edwards
Swan Hill
April 2003

1
Introduction – What's the Big Idea?

Set into the wall of the Church of the Ascension on London's Blackheath is a small metal plaque. 'Fellowship is life', it reads, 'and lack of fellowship is death, but in hell there is no brotherhood but every man for himself.' John Ball, the leader of the Peasants' Revolt who spoke these words nearby in 1381, would not have thought of himself as part of 'civil society', but his sentiments have been echoed down the centuries by anyone who has ever joined a group, formed an association or volunteered to defend or advance the causes they believe in. Collective action in search of the good society is a universal part of human experience, though manifested in a million different ways across time, space and culture. In Sullivan County, New York, where I spend my weekends, I am surrounded by contemporary examples of this same phenomenon – the volunteer fire service, the free give-away of hay to those who can't afford to buy it for their pets, the music sale by Radio W-JEFF ('America's only hydro-powered public radio station'), the Interfaith Council Peace Vigil in nearby Liberty, the local HIV/Aids Taskforce and a myriad of groups catering to every conceivable affinity and interest. Yet Sullivan County remains economically depressed and politically forgotten, one more set of communities on the margins of a nation that is increasingly violent, unequal and apparently incapable of resolving its own pressing social problems. A strong civil society, it seems, is no guarantee that society will be strong and civil.

Concepts of civil society have a rich history, but it is only in the last ten years that they have moved to the centre of the international stage. There are a number of reasons for this – the fall of Communism and the democratic openings that followed, disenchantment with the economic models of the past, a yearning for togetherness in a world that seems evermore insecure, and the rapid rise of non-governmental organizations (NGOs) on the global stage. Today, civil society seems to be the 'big idea' on everyone's lips – government officials, journalists, funding agencies, writers and academics, not to mention the millions of people across the globe who find it an inspiration in their struggles for a better world. Cited as a solution to social, economic and political dilemmas by politicians and thinkers from left, right and all perspectives in between, civil society is claimed by every part of the ideological spectrum as its own, but what exactly is it?

'Civil society', says the libertarian Cato Institute in Washington DC, means 'fundamentally reducing the role of politics in society by expanding free markets and individual liberty.'[1] Don Eberly, a leading conservative thinker, goes even further: 'As the twenty-first century draws near', he says, 'a new term has surfaced in American political debate, carrying with it all of the collective longing of a nation looking for a new direction. That term is civil society.' This will surprise those on the left who see it as the seedbed for radical social movements. The Advocacy Institute, one of Cato's alter-egos, calls civil society 'the best way forward for politics in the post-Cold War world', 'a society that protects those who organize to challenge power' and 'the single most viable alternative to the authoritarian state and the tyrannical market'.[2] Not to be outdone, 'third way' thinkers like Anthony Giddens and Benjamin Barber claim that civil society – by gently correcting generations of state and market failure – could be the missing link in the success of social democracy. Meanwhile back in academia, civil society has become the 'chicken soup of the social sciences', and 'the new analytic key that will unlock the mysteries of the social order'. The American writer Jeremy Rifkin calls civil society 'our last, best hope'; New Labour politicians in the UK see it as central to a new 'project' that will hold society together against the onrush of globalizing markets; the United Nations and the World Bank see it as one of the keys to 'good gov- ernance' and poverty-reducing growth; and – lest one sees this as a giant Western conspiracy – here is the autumn 2002 edition of China's semi-official news magazine '*Huasheng Shidian*' plagiarizing American civil society scholar Lester Salamon: 'the role of NGOs in the twenty-first century will be as significant as the role of the nation state in the twentieth'. These are strange bedfellows with ambitious dreams, but can they all be right?

Such chameleon-like qualities are not unique to 'civil society', but when the same phrase is used to justify such radically different viewpoints it is certainly time to ask some deeper questions about what is going on. An idea that means everything probably means nothing, and when the idea of civil society goes on sale to the highest bidder, its worth as a political and intellectual currency is likely to be devalued over time. At the very least, clarity about the different under- standings in play is necessary if we are to a have a sensible conversation, yet a glance through the civil society literature would leave most people rapidly and thoroughly confused. Depending on whose version one follows, civil society is either a specific product of the nation state and capitalism (arising spontaneously to mediate conflicts between social life and the market economy when the industrial revolution fractured traditional bonds of kin and community), or a uni- versal expression of the collective life of individuals, at work in all countries and stages of development but expressed in different ways according to history and context. Since nation states in the developing world are largely a colonial creation and the market economy has only a fragile hold, civil soci- eties in the South are bound to differ from those in the North. Some see civil society as one of three sectors (along with the state and the market), separate from and independent of each other though overlapping in the middle. Others emphasize the 'fuzzy' borders and interrelationships that exist between these sectors, characterized by hybrids, connections and overlaps between different institutions and their roles. Some claim that only certain associations are part of civil society – voluntary, democratic, modern and 'civil' according to some pre-defined set of normative criteria. Others insist that all associations qualify for membership, including 'uncivil' society and traditional associations based on inherited characteristics like religion and ethnicity. Are families 'in' or 'out', and what about the business sector? Is civil society a bulwark against the state, an indispensable support or dependent on government intervention for its very existence? Is it the key to individual freedom through the guaranteed experience of pluralism or a threat to democracy through special interest politics? Is it a noun (a part of society), an adjective (a kind of society), an arena for societal deliberation or a mixture of all three?

It is not difficult to find support for any of these positions, and we will hear much more about the different arguments later in the book. But what is to be done with a concept that seems so unsure of itself that definitions are akin to nailing jelly to the wall? One response would be to ditch the concept completely, as recently recommended by John Grimond in *The Economist* magazine. 'Civil society' appears as one of five leading articles in its flagship publication *The World In 2002*, only to be dismissed as a smokescreen for the 'usual suspects' (meaning 'NGOs and their self-selected agendas') and a 'woolly expression for woolly-minded people' – except, Grimond adds in case his message appears too nuanced, that this 'would be too charitable'. Though tempting, this would be a serious mistake, since although the civil society debate is 'riddled with ethnocentric assumptions developed in conditions that don't exist anywhere in the contemporary world', is 'no longer based on any coherent theory or principles', has been reduced to 'an ideological rendezvous for erstwhile antagonists', and is therefore 'ineffective as a model for social and political practice', the concept itself is very much alive and kicking in the worlds of politics, activism and foreign aid.[3] Therefore, 'the resultant intellectual confusion could well wreak havoc on the real world given the fact that civil societies have now been recognized as a legitimate area for external intervention.'[4] Analytical rigour, conceptual clarity, empirical authenticity, policy relevance and emancipatory potential are all threatened when civil society becomes a slogan. But selective scorn, scholarly admonishment and attempts to enforce a universal consensus are unlikely to resolve this problem, now that such ideas have developed a life of their own, backed by powerful interests.

What, therefore, is the best way forward? I think it lies through rigour, since rigour enables different interpretations to be debated on their merits and demerits in the court of public deliberation. Without clarity and rigour, theories of civil society will be a poor guide to public policy and citizen action, whatever the values and goals at stake. At the very least, rigour can expose dogma that masquerades as truth, and challenge policy makers who have an ideological axe to grind. And, as I try to show in the chapters that follow, ideas about civil society can survive and prosper in a rigorous critique so long as we are prepared to abandon false universals, magic bullets and painless panaceas. The goal of this book is not consensus (something that would be impossible to achieve in the civil society debate), but greater clarity. And greater clarity, I hope, can be the basis for a better conversation in the future.

Civil society: a very brief history of an idea

The first step in achieving greater clarity is to identify the origins of different contemporary understandings of civil society in the history of political thought. This is not a theoretical book, nor a book about civil society theory, but to appreciate the ways in which theory has been muddled and misapplied in practice a quick tour through theory is essential. As Keynes's famous dictum reminds us, 'practical men in authority who think themselves immune from theoretical influences are usually the slaves of some defunct economist', just as present-day 'civil-society builders' are motivated, consciously or not, by ideas that are deeply rooted in the past.

Fortunately, we are blessed with a number of books that already provide excellent and detailed accounts of the history of this idea.[5] They show how civil society has been a point of reference for philosophers since antiquity in their struggle to understand the great issues of the day: the nature of the good society, the rights and responsibilities of citizens, the practice of politics and government, and, most especially, how to live together peacefully by reconciling our individual autonomy with our collective aspirations, balancing freedom and its boundaries, and marrying pluralism with conformity so that complex societies can function with both efficiency and justice. Such questions were difficult enough to resolve in small, homogenous communities where face-to-face social interaction built trust and reciprocity, but in an increasingly integrated world where none of these conditions apply they become hugely more demanding. Yet the discussions that took place in the ferment of eastern Europe in the 1980s would surely have been familiar to Aristotle, Hobbes, Ferguson, de Tocqueville, Gramsci and others in the long roster of civil society thinkers that stretches back two thousand years. Though the profile of these ideas has certainly waxed and waned, arguing about civil society has always been a part of political and philosophical debate.

In classical thought, civil society and the state were seen as indistinguishable, with both referring to a type of political association governing social conflict through the imposition of rules that restrained citizens from harming one another. Aristotle's *polis* was an 'association of associations' that enabled citizens (or those few individuals that qualified) to share in the virtuous tasks of ruling and being ruled. In this sense, the state represented the 'civil' form of society and 'civility' described the requirements of good citizenship. Late medieval thought continued this tradition by equating civil society with 'politically-organized commonwealths', a type of civilization made possible because people lived in law-governed associations protected *by* the state.[6] The alternative, as Thomas Hobbes pointed out in his *Leviathan*, was 'survival of the fittest'.

Between 1750 and 1850, ideas about civil society took a new and fundamental turn in response to a perceived crisis in the ruling social order. This crisis was motivated by the rise of the market economy and the increasing differentiation of interests it provoked, as 'communities of strangers' replaced 'communities of neighbours'; and by the breakdown of traditional paradigms of authority as a consequence of the French and American revolutions. In contrast to Aristotle, Plato and Hobbes, the thinkers of the Enlightenment viewed civil society as a defence against unwarranted intrusions by the state on newly realized individual rights and freedoms, organized through the medium of voluntary associations. In this school of thought, civil society was a self-regulating universe of associations committed to the same ideals that needed, at all costs, to be protected *from* the state in order to preserve its role in resisting despotism. This was a theme taken up by a host of thinkers including James Madison (in his *Federalist Papers*), Alexis de Tocqueville (probably the most famous civil society enthusiast of them all), and – much later in time – by the 'small circles of freedom' formed by dissidents in eastern Europe, by the writers who celebrated them in the West (like Ernest Gellner), and by academics such as Robert Putnam who began to investigate the condition of associational life and its effects in Italy, the USA and elsewhere, spawning a whole new debate on 'social capital' in the process. The dominant theme in this debate was the value of voluntary associations in curbing the power of centralizing institutions, protecting pluralism and nurturing constructive social norms, especially 'generalized trust and cooperation'. A highly articulated civil society with overlapping memberships was seen as the foundation of a stable democratic polity, a defence against domination by any one group, and a barrier to anti-democratic forces.[7]

Today, this 'neo-Tocquevillian' tradition is particularly strong in the USA, where it dovetails naturally with pre-existing traditions of self-governance, suspicions about the state, and concerns about public disengagement from politics and civic life, and is closely linked to other schools of thought such as communitarianism, localism and the 'liberal egalitarianism' of Michael Walzer, William Galston and others.[8] In contrast to classical liberals, liberal egalitarians recognize the debilitating effects of unequal access to resources and opportunities on the health and functioning of civil society. This is an important insight, and scholars have built on these ideas to construct a comprehensive critique of the neo-Tocquevillian tradition that focuses on the structural obstacles that prevent some groups from articulating their interests, the ethnocentrism or simple unreliability of assumptions about associations and their effects, and a failure to account for the impact of globalization, economic restructuring, political corruption and power relations of different kinds.[9] Even this critique, however, reaches back through history to connect with much earlier debates about the ideas that developed during the Enlightenment. Hegel was the first of these early critics, focusing on the conflicts and inequalities that raged between different economic and political interests within civil society that required constant surveillance by the state in order for the 'civil' to remain. This was a theme taken further by Karl Marx, who saw civil society as another vehicle for furthering the interests of the dominant class under capitalism, and then by Antonio Gramsci – the person who 'may be single-handedly responsible for the revival of the term civil society in the post-World War Two period'.[10] Although Gramsci reasoned in Marxist categories, he reached some conclusions that differed from his intellectual master, since in Gramsci's view, civil society was the site of rebellion against the orthodox as well as the construction of cultural and ideological hegemony, expressed through families, schools, universities and the media as well as voluntary associations since all these institutions are important in shaping the political dispositions of citizens.

Philosophers in the United States such as John Dewey and Hannah Arendt took Gramsci's ideas about civil society as an arena for contestation and developed around them a theory of the 'public sphere' as an essential component of democracy. By the 'public', Dewey meant the shared experience of political life that underpinned public deliberation on the great questions of the day. Anything that eroded this public sphere – like the commercialization of the media or the commodification of education – was to be resisted. Such ideas continue to resonate today among Americans committed to 'deliberative democracy', but it was in Europe that the theory of the public sphere reached its highest levels of articulation through the work of Jürgen Habermas. Habermas combined the Marxist tradition that exposes domination in civil society with the liberal tradition that emphasizes its role in guarding personal autonomy, and drew these different threads together through a complicated series of theoretical constructs concerning 'communicative action', 'discursive democracy' and the 'colonization of the life world'. For Habermas and other 'critical theorists', a healthy civil society is one 'that is steered by its members through shared meanings' that are constructed democratically through the communications structures of the public sphere.[11] Today, these ideas are echoed by theorists and activists on the left who see civil society as the site of progressive politics – 'the social basis of a democratic public sphere through which a culture of inequality can be dismantled' – and by political philosophers like John Keane who are attempting to construct a new vision of civil society that respects differences between groups by promoting non-violent engagement 'from above' (through state authority embedded in national constitutions and international law) and 'from below' (by channelling violent tendencies into non-violent associational life).[12]

This whistle-stop tour through history shows that ideas about civil society have passed through many phases without ever securing a consensus, even leaving aside all the other variants of civil society thinking that I have omitted in order to focus on the basics – such as non-Western theories or theories about non-Western societies, scholarship about African-American civil society in the USA, feminist contributions to the debate and others. I will get to these contributions a little later, though most of my analysis will be skewed towards North America and western Europe, and the literatures they have spawned. Although work on civil society outside these contexts is growing, it has not yet reached a level at which systematic comparisons can be made, including the notion of 'global' civil society, a concept much in vogue but little interrogated by its enthusiasts. Nevertheless, there is little doubt that the civil society debate will continue to divide scholars in fundamental ways, and although such divisions are never watertight, I want to focus in the rest of the book on three contrasting schools of thought that emerge from this brief discussion of the history of ideas: civil society as a *part* of society (the neo-Toquevillian school that focuses on associational life), civil society as a *kind* of society (characterized by positive norms and values as well as success in meeting particular social goals), and civil society as the *public sphere*. After exploring each of these schools in detail, the latter part of the book shows how they are related to each other, and where such an integrated approach might lead in terms of public policy.

Each of these three schools of thought has a respectable intellectual history and is visible in the discourse of scholars, politicians, foundations and international agencies, but it is the first – civil society as associational life – that is dominant. It is Alexis de Tocqueville's ghost that wanders through the corridors of the World Bank, not that of Habermas or Hegel. Indeed, the first two schools of thought are regularly conflated – it being assumed that a healthy associational life contributes to, or even produces, the 'good society' in predictable ways – while the public sphere is usually ignored. This messy mélange of means and ends will be challenged extensively in the pages that follow, but before embarking on this investigation it is important to understand why such lazy thinking is so common. Why has this particular interpretation of civil society become so popular since the Cold War ended?

The rise and rise of civil society

There is no doubt that neo-Tocquevillian ideas about civil society have been a prime beneficiary of wider political and ideological changes that have redefined the powers and responsibilities of states, markets and voluntary associations over the last twenty years. At the broadest level, there are three ways in which societies can organize collective action – through rules or laws enforced by the coercive power of the state, through the unintended consequences of individual decisions in the marketplace, and through social mechanisms embedded in voluntary action, discussion and agreement. The weight attached to each of these models has shifted significantly over the last fifty years, with state-based solutions in the ascendancy from 1945 to the mid-1970s (the era of the welfare state in the North and centralized planning in the South), and market-based solutions in pole position from the late 1970s to 1990 or thereabouts (the era of Reaganomics in the North and 'structural adjustment' in the South). Disaffection with the results of both these models – the deadening effect of too much state intervention and the human consequences of an over-reliance on the market – required a new approach that addressed the consequences of both state and market failure. This new approach, which gained strength throughout the 1990s, went by many names (including the 'third way', the 'new localism' and 'compassionate conservatism'), but its central tenet is that partnership between all three 'sectors' of society working together – public, private and civic – is the best way to overcome social and economic problems. Civil society as associational life became central to the workings of this project, and this project – as a new way of achieving social progress – became identified with building 'societies that are civil'.

In addition, the political changes that culminated in the fall of the Berlin Wall in 1989 gave the idea of civil society a prominence it had not enjoyed since the Enlightenment, but in a manner that also encouraged the conflation of ends with means. Civil society became both a rallying cry for dissidents – a new type of society characterized by liberal-democratic norms – and a vehicle for achieving it by building social movements strong enough to overthrow authoritarian states. The paradigm case for the conflation of these two perspectives was Solidarity in Poland, though here as elsewhere in eastern Europe, associational life tended to be disregarded fairly quickly once the dissidents were elected into office. Nevertheless, the rise of direct democracy that was such a feature of political change in eastern Europe, the former Soviet Union and large parts of the developing world during the 1990s remains a trend of global importance, perhaps as important as the invention of representative democracy in the eighteenth and nineteenth centuries. As the balance between direct and representative democracy continues to shift in favour of the former – driven by disaffection with conventional politics as well as the attractions of alternative means of participation – the political role of voluntary associations (as the prime vehicles for organizing such participation) will continue to grow. As we shall see in later chapters, this role is fraught with difficulty both for voluntary associations and for the processes of politics, but it seems unlikely that the trend itself will be reversed.

Worldwide moves towards state retrenchment and privatization (even with the humanizing touches now applied by civil society) have promoted new levels of personal insecurity among the majority of the world's population against a background of global market integration, increased mobility of people and capital, and rapid social and technological change. Modernity, as Robert Bellah reminds us, is a 'culture of separation', while capitalism provides no collective identity to bring us together other than as consumers.[13] Traditional social institutions and ways of dealing with such insecurities (like welfare states, labour unions and nuclear families) have been progressively dismantled during this process, leaving behind heightened levels of uncertainty and vulnerability. In these circumstances, a retreat to the familiar is to be expected, and this is exactly what voluntary associations can provide – a reassuring oasis of solidarity and mutual support among like-minded people who provide each other with emotional as well as material support, from soup kitchens to self-help to spiritual salvation. Indeed, an additional reason for the rapid rise in interest in civil society over the last decade has been the collection of a mounting body of evidence that suggests that associational life plays a much more important social, economic and political role than was realized in the 1970s and 1980s. Civil society has been noticed, not just because of the rising public and political profile of NGOs and other groups, but because a body of evidence now exists to justify this profile, backed by specialist expertise in universities and think-tanks and supported with large amounts of money from research funding bodies, foundations and governments.

At the level of national development performance, this evidence shows that the synergy between a strong state and a strong society is one of the keys to sustained, poverty-reducing growth, because networks of intermediary associations act as a counterweight to vested interests, promote institutional accountability among states and markets, channel information to decision-makers on what is happening at the 'sharp end', and negotiate the social contracts between government and citizens that development requires – 'I'll scratch your back by delivering growth, investment and services; you scratch mine by delivering wage restraint or absorbing the costs of welfare.' Taiwan, one of the most successful of late industrializers, had over 8 million members in such intermediary groups by the early 1980s, including trade unions, student associations and local councils.[14]

At a more detailed level, it is useful to break down the developmental roles of civil society into three interrelated areas: economic, political and social. The economic role of civil society centres on securing livelihoods and providing services where states and markets are weak, and nurturing the social values, networks and institutions that underpin successful market economies, including trust and cooperation. As Lester Salamon and his colleagues have shown, voluntary associations the world over have become key providers of human services (especially health and welfare), and now constitute a 1.1 *trillion* dollar industry.[15] NGOs, religious organizations and other civic groups have always been significant service-providers; the difference now is that they are seen as the preferred channel for service provision in deliberate substitution for the state. In more radical formulations (like the World Social Forum), civil society is seen as a vehicle for 'humanizing capitalism' by promoting accountability among corporations, progressive social policies (like respect for labour rights) among governments, and new experiments in 'social economics' that combine market efficiency with cooperative values.

In their social role, civil societies are seen as a reservoir of caring, cultural life and intellectual innovation, teaching people – at least according to the neo-Tocquevillians – the skills of citizenship and nurturing a collection of positive social norms that foster stability, loosely collected under the rubric of 'social capital'. In turn, social capital is seen as the crucial ingredient in promoting collective action for the common good, or simply creating and maintaining the social ties that are essential if individuals are to function effectively in modern economies where the demands of exchange grow increasingly complex. The normative effects of voluntary associations lie at the core of the neo-Tocquevillian argument, though this is as much a moral as a social issue for them. In some ways this is to be expected, since many neo-Tocquevillians are conservatives and conservatives tend to look back in time to recreate what they consider to be the best of times, defined according to a particular set of moral standards. Liberals and social democrats, on the other hand, tend to look forward to better times to come, so they pay more attention to civil society as a vehicle for creating new solutions. The relative marginalization of theories of the public sphere is partly explained by the current ascendancy of conservatives and conservative thinking in Western politics.

In their political role, voluntary associations are seen as a crucial counterweight to states and corporate power, and an essential pillar in promoting transparency, accountability and other aspects of 'good governance', the favourite term of foreign-aid donors in recent times. Especially where formal citizenship rights are not well entrenched, it is civil society that provides the channels through which most people can make their voices heard in government decision-making, protect and promote their civil and political rights, and strengthen their skills as future political leaders. Arguing from democratic theory, a strong civil society can prevent the agglomeration of power that threatens autonomy and choice, provide effective checks against the abuse of state authority, and protect a democratic public sphere in which citizens can debate the ends and means of governance. The role of NGOs and social movements in mobilizing opposition to authoritarian rule and supporting progress towards multi-party elections has been well documented in Africa, eastern Europe and Latin America.[16] Over the last five years these functions have been extended to the global level, with NGO networks becoming increasingly influential in challenging the policies of the international financial institutions and establishing new norms of accountability. Civil society in this sense means 'people power' writ large.

On the surface at least, these arguments provide powerful support for the associational view of civil society. It would be disingenuous, however, to argue that official support for civil society is based purely on the findings of research. The fact that such support is 'good for business', as I have put it elsewhere, is also important.[17] By this I don't mean the business sector (though recent moves by corporations to cosy up to NGOs is another illustration of this trend), but any attempt by official institutions to develop 'legitimacy by association' with citizens' groups which enjoy much higher levels of public trust. Developing positive relationships with civil society groups has become an essential 'pre-defence' against attacks from the same sector. Both the World Bank and the specialized agencies of the United Nations are opening their doors, slowly, to civil society groups in this fashion, and the political costs of retreating into the bunker would likely be considerable in terms of their public image and support. Such trends raise the dangers of co-optation, of course, especially when NGOs already worry that 'support for civil society' means 'privatization by stealth', signifying the use of voluntary associations as a smokescreen for state retrenchment and corporate interests.

Since 2000, there have been signs that these high levels of interest and support are waning, confirming Alan Wolfe's judgement that the 'idea of civil society failed because it became too popular'.[18] 'Civil society is passé' was the conclusion of a senior German government official in private conversation recently, 'it had its moment in the 1990s but now it's time to move on to something else.'[19] Some of these critiques have been intelligent and helpful, reaffirming the practical value of voluntary associations but rejecting the 'conceits of civil society' as Neera Chandoke puts it, meaning exaggerated notions of their political importance or ability to replace the nation state (a fantasy akin to 'grasping at straws' according to David Rieff).[20] Others have been knee-jerk reactions to anti-globalization protests such as the 'battle of Seattle' and the skirmishes that followed – charges against NGOs as 'the leftover left' and 'loonies and paranoids', for example, that have graced the pages of *Newsweek* and *Time*.[21] There are a number of reasons for this backlash, including fears from governments in the South that NGOs may be replacing the state in many parts of sub-Saharan Africa and south Asia; confusion about 'who belongs' in civil society after the al-Qaeda attacks on New York and Washington DC on 11 September 2001; worries about NGO performance, legitimacy, accountability and dependence on foreign funding; concerns among trade unions that NGOs have hijacked the name and functions of civil society for a narrow set of purposes and constituencies; public reactions against street violence among 'anti-globalization' protestors; and well-publicized cases of corruption in major charities.[22] Overall, however, these criticisms are helpful since they remind us that civil society is, and should continue to be, the subject of debate, in part because any institution that grows in influence must also be subjected to external pressure for accountability (NGOs now constitute a 'fifth estate' according to a recent worldwide opinion poll).[23]

It is no longer possible to regard civil society as the preserve of a subset of privileged individuals – the citizens of the Greek *polis*, white male property-owners in eighteenth-century Europe, or the West, the North or the South. The idea of civil society has spread across the world to become a powerful leitmotif in politics and practice, yet it remains dominated by a narrow and disputed interpretation of what civil society is and does, and this narrowness threatens to erode its potential as a force for positive social change. Preserving this potential requires a simultaneous broadening of the debate to include other, less dominant, perspectives, and a much greater specification of what each of these perspectives has to contribute to a clearer understanding overall. And the starting point for that process is to break apart the assumptions that underpin the orthodox interpretation of civil society as the world of associational life.

2
Civil Society as Associational Life

In the late thirteenth century, Marco Polo was struck by the vibrancy of associational life in the Chinese city of Hangzhou, 'noted for its charitable institutions as for its pleasures'.[1] Public hospitals, market associations, free cemeteries, cultural groups and homes for the elderly abounded. No doubt earlier explorers would have seen similar things on their travels too, since associations like these have existed from at least the days of the Pharaohs. Human beings (or most of us at least) are social creatures, and joining groups that help us to resolve the problems of collective action (like water-users' associations in south Asia), advance the causes we believe in (like Amnesty International), find more meaning and fulfilment in life (like religious groups) or simply have some fun (like the choirs and bowling clubs beloved of Robert Putnam) is a universal part of human experience. A life lived without such opportunities would be severely – perhaps unremittingly – diminished. For some, voluntary association is the natural state of humankind, invested with almost spiritual significance. 'Human beings', writes J. Ronald Engel, 'are made for the life of free association, and that divine reality, the Holy Spirit, is manifest in all associations committed to the democratic pursuit of justice in the common life.'[2] Such attitudes are especially common in the

USA, where the health and vitality of associations are often taken – at least by Americans – as the 'envy of the world'.[3] It was Alexis de Tocqueville that started this romance on his travels to the USA in the 1830s. 'Americans of all ages, conditions and dispositions', he declared in a now-famous passage from his book, *Democracy in America*, 'have a constant tendency to form associations.'[4] Today, almost 800,000 Americans are members of volunteer fire brigades, for example (constituting 73 per cent of all fire-fighters in the country), something that is as quintessentially American as the bucket brigade and hand truck in centuries gone by.

This love affair has stirred passions on all sides of the political spectrum. Conservatives see associations as vehicles for rebuilding traditional moral values, while progressives see them as vehicles for rebuilding whole societies, and the world. Yet does this mean that voluntary action is always the best way to run a fire service, or reform society? As long ago as 1911, Max Weber warned against romanticizing the effects of associations in his address to a congress of sociologists in Frankfurt: 'the man of today is without doubt an association man in an awful and never dreamed of degree', he said, citing the negative effects on political engagement of the singing societies that were proliferating across Germany at the time – a fascinating anticipation of contemporary critiques of those like Putnam who praise the positive civic and political effects of choirs.[5] Associations matter hugely and should be encouraged, but there is equal danger in expecting too much from associational life, as if it were a 'magic bullet' for resolving the intractable social, economic and political problems surveyed in brief in chapter 1. Increasingly, it seems, voluntary associations are expected to organize social services, govern local communities, solve the unemployment problem, save the environment, and still have time left over for rebuilding the moral life of nations. 'Don't ask us to carry more than our capacity and then blame failure on us', says the Peruvian NGO leader Mario Padron, 'we can't carry the load.'[6]

This chapter focuses on civil society as a *part* of society that is distinct from states and markets, the most common of the understandings in use today and the direct descendant of de Tocqueville's ideas about nineteenth-century America. Commonly referred to as the 'third' or 'non-profit' sector, civil society in this sense contains all associations and networks between the family and the state in which membership and activities are 'voluntary' – formally registered NGOs of many different kinds, labour unions, political parties, churches and other religious groups, professional and business associations, community and self-help groups, social movements and the independent media. This is the 'space of un-coerced human association' in Michael Walzer's famous definition, 'and also the set of relational networks – formed for the sake of family, faith, interest and ideology – that fill this space'.[7] The word 'voluntary' here needs a little explication, since many such associations are run by paid professionals as well as volunteers. The key criteria are that membership is consensual rather than legally required, meaning that 'exit is possible without loss of status or public rights or benefits', and that voluntaristic mechanisms are used to achieve objectives, meaning dialogue, bargaining and persuasion instead of enforced compliance by governments or market incentives by firms.[8] Whether such associations attract at least some voluntary contributions of time and/or money is a useful additional test. Nevertheless, as John Keane points out, 'civil society is an *ideal-typical category . . . that both describes and envisages* a complex and dynamic ensemble of legally-protected non-governmental institutions that tend to be non-violent, self-organizing, self-reflexive and permanently in tension with each other and with the state institutions that frame, construct and enable their activities'.[9] The reality of associational life is much more complicated than this 'ideal' suggests.

Is there an 'associational revolution' at work in the world today?

Voluntary associations have existed in most parts of the world for hundreds of years. The rural peasants' cooperatives that sprang into action after the French Revolution, for example; the 'Young Men's Lyceum' in Springfield, Illinois, where Abraham Lincoln first practised his oratory in 1838; the nineteenth-century reform movements like Araya Samaj that pre-dated mass political action in India; and – despite the risks involved – the many dissident groups that remained active in eastern Europe throughout Communist rule. Over the last ten years, however, the expansion of some forms of associational life has been so rapid and so global that commentators have begun to talk of an 'associational revolution' or a 'power shift' of potentially momentous significance.[10] Except in a small number of cases where authoritarian governments still block the development of voluntary associations on principle – like Myanmar (Burma) and Cuba – the numbers of registered non-profit organizations have increased at rates not seen before in history, especially in developing countries, which started from a lower base and received large amounts of foreign aid for investment in new and existing NGOs.

For example, the number of registered NGOs in Nepal increased from 220 in 1990 to 1,210 in 1993; in Bolivia from 100 in 1980 to 530 in 1992; and in Tunisia from 1,886 in 1988 to 5,186 in 1991.[11] The largest-ever survey of the non-profit sector in twenty-two countries found over 1 million such organizations in India by 1997, 210,000 in Brazil, 17,500 in Egypt and 15,000 in Thailand. According to the same survey, the non-profit sector in these countries accounted for one in every twelve jobs and almost 11 million volunteers. In Ghana, Zimbabwe and Kenya, the sector provides 40 per cent or more of all healthcare and education services delivered. And even in China, where government policy remains suspicious, the number of registered national non-profit organizations increased to around 2,000 by 2001. Paralleling this increase in numbers has been the growth of individual NGOs to cover the provision of services to millions of people, especially in south Asia – over 2 million in the case of the Bangladesh Rural Advancement Committee, for example, over 1 million for the Self-Employed Women's Association in India, and over 7,000 villages in the case of Sarvodaya in Sri Lanka. Social movements like the movement of the landless in Brazil (with over 300,000 members and 20,000 'core activists' by 2002) have also grown apace.

In western Europe and the USA the pattern is more complex, with claims and counter-claims about the rise and fall of different types of association since the Second World War. Robert Putnam has built his reputation on the thesis that civic engagement in America as a whole has declined, though he recognizes that national non-profit organizations have increased from 10,299 in 1968 to almost 23,000 in 1997, as has membership in professional associations (at least in absolute terms), religious groups and small self-help groups (like Alcoholics Anonymous), and volunteering, especially among young people.[12] The Sierra Club grew from 114,000 members in 1970 to over 550,000 in 1996, and Greenpeace from a mere 250 members in 1971 to 1.7 million twenty-five years later. In contrast, membership in traditional mass-based organizations (like parent–teacher associations) and labour unions has declined significantly (by as much as 62 per cent in manufacturing and 78 per cent in construction). This analysis – that the shape of US civil society is changing – is also accepted by Putnam's critics, in terms of the facts of what is happening if not the gloomy interpretation of their implications. A similar pattern is evident in the UK, where 'mutual aid' associations and labour unions have declined since 1945 but NGOs and advocacy groups have grown substantially: Friends of the Earth, for example, increased its membership from 75,000 in 1988 to 200,000 in 1995, while Amnesty International's membership grew from 39,000 in 1987 to 108,300 five years later.[13]

At the international level, a new layer of NGOs and NGO networks has emerged over the last ten years to constitute a 'global civil society', or at least a transnational NGO community. Over 40,000 international NGOs and 20,000 transnational NGO networks are already active on the world stage, 90 per cent of which have been formed since 1970.[14] They include famous names like Oxfam and Save the Children, successful campaigns like Jubilee 2000 on debt relief, global movements like the Hemispheric Social Alliance (which already claims to have 49 million 'members'), federations of community groups like Shack Dwellers International that links hundreds of thousands of people across three continents, and international associations of mayors, local authorities, business representatives, professionals, universities and writers.

However, despite this avalanche of figures we are left with only one unambiguous fact about trends in associational life worldwide: the numbers of formally registered non-governmental organizations have risen substantially since 1989. Every other important piece of information is disputed, either by evidence from different countries or cultures, by opinions from different schools of thought or ideological positions, or by those who discount the NGO phenomenon as a temporary 'blip' in world affairs that has been promoted by foreign aid during a time when civil society has been in fashion. Because the data for most of the world cover only registered organizations, trends in other areas of associational life are difficult to identify, especially those below the radar screen of academic research like community groups and grassroots movements. We do not know whether past developments are a reliable guide to the future (especially once NGOs are forced to rely on money raised from their own societies, not from foreign aid), and scholars cannot agree on what the broader implications of these trends might be. An 'associational revolution' or 'power shift' would surely signal structural changes in politics, economics and social relations, not just an increase in the numbers and size of NGOs at work on the margins. In any case, it makes no sense to lump all non-profit organizations into a single category of 'associational life', from the Ford Foundation to a burial society in South Africa, or to fixate – as the foreign-aid community has done – on NGOs as the most important type of association among so many. The first source of disagreement concerns the thorny issue of which associations belong in civil society, and which do not.

Who is 'in' and who is 'out'?

The three-sector model of society implies that states, markets and non-profit groups are separate from and independent of each other – hermetically sealed, perhaps, in their own rationalities and particular ways of working. Yet even a glimpse at real institutions demonstrates that this is nonsense. Boundaries are always 'fuzzy' or fluid, and there are reasons why this is necessarily so – I, like you, am simultaneously citizen, neighbour, worker and consumer, and the qualities developed in one of these roles spill over into the others, one hopes with positive effects. Civil society and the state, for example, have always been interdependent, with states providing the legal and regulatory framework a democratic civil society needs to function, and civil society exerting the pressure for accountability that keeps elected governments on track. As Theda Skocpol has shown, effective US social policies between 1945 and 1980 worked through symbiotic ties that developed between government and locally rooted membership associations.[15] This does not, of course, mean that civil society is part of the state or vice versa – they are clearly different sets of institutions – but if they are disconnected then the positive effects of each on the other can be negated. Whether states have more influence over civil society or civil societies over states has been a source of disagreement among scholars for 200 years or more, but clearly government policy can have a major impact on the strength and shape of associational life – think of attacks on the labour movement by Ronald Reagan and Margaret Thatcher, or in more positive vein, the encouragement of non-profit-sector service provision under 'New Labour' in Britain or Democratic and Republican administrations in the USA. However, if these links become too close and cosy, then governments can be captured by particular sets of interests in civil society (some examples are given below) and civil society may be unable to play its watchdog role on government. State institutions, therefore, cannot be part of associational life.

Sitting between associations and the state, however, is a grey area called 'political society' – meaning parties, political organizations and parliaments – that has divided civil society scholars into two rival camps. The first camp sees political society as a crucial component of civil society, not because civic groups seek state power (they don't) or aggregate the interests of individuals into political settlements (they can't), but because they generate influence on politics through the life of democratic associations and unconstrained discussion in the public sphere. 'In the long run, democratic political societies depend for their health on the depth of their roots in independent pre-political associations and publics.'[16] Solidarity in Poland was both a labour union and a political party in waiting, and social movements usually have implicit political agendas. In Rajasthan, for example, the Mazdoor Kisan Shakti Sangathan, a 'non-party political formation' that works with workers' and peasants' groups, has already fielded candidates in local elections and is considering entering the race for office at the state level too.[17] In countries like Indonesia with weak multi-party systems (or where parties are forbidden at the local level), alliances between national political formations on the one hand, and peasant movements and labour unions at the local and regional levels on the other, are developing rapidly.[18] South Africa's Treatment Action Campaign began as an alliance of NGOs determined to change government policy on retroviral drugs for HIV/Aids patients, but is now developing some of the characteristics of an opposition against the background of rule by the African National Congress, but without a formal political identity. And leaders in countries like Chile, the Philippines and Brazil under President Lula move regularly from NGOs to government and back. So linkages between civil and political society are natural, useful and to be encouraged, especially at a time when the balance between direct and representative democracy is changing in favour of the former.

The second camp shudders at the corrupting influence of politics on associations, since associations are assumed to be independent of any partisan political interests. If they weren't independent, they wouldn't be able to play the role that is claimed for them in cementing 'generalized' trust and tolerance across different political communities and promoting a genuine sense of the 'common interest'. Putnam and other neo-Toquevillians accept that apolitical associations can have political effects because of their influence on overall levels of political participation, including voting, though the evidence for and against this proposition is contested.[19] However, this is not the same as formal political activity, and there are certainly examples of the damage that can be done when voluntary associations formally ally themselves with parties competing for votes. ADAB (the association of NGOs in Bangladesh), for example, joined forces with the Awami League in 1996, leading to new forms of patron–client relationships once the league had been elected into office.[20] In the USA, religious conservatives (through the Christian Coalition of America) represent approximately 18 per cent of the electorate, and regularly use their connections with senior Republicans on Capitol Hill and in the White House to influence public policy on reproductive rights, foreign policy, federal aid to faith-based organizations and other issues too. Similar examples, of course, could be cited from the Democrats, but that is not the point – any association that claims to promote the public interest is in dangerous water when it allies itself with a partisan political agenda. At the very least it might lose its favourable tax status; more importantly, it may forfeit its claims to represent the broader agenda of citizens in civil society. 'We're sick of politics' is a familiar refrain among community groups and volunteers.

For many, while trust may be the lubricant of civil society, hypocrisy is the Vaseline of political influence.

There has always been a strong strain of 'anti politics', as George Konrad calls it, among civil society enthusiasts, driven partly by the belief that civil society can organize and govern itself successfully without the need for government intervention, or government at all in the conventional sense of the word. This may be true at the scale of a New England town meeting, but it is unlikely to be effective at the national level, and even less in global regimes, despite the increasing importance of direct democracy in 'filling out' the processes of politics. Indeed, at global level these questions are even more complex because so few formal political structures exist across national boundaries to arbitrate between different interests – structures such as parties, parliaments, accountability mechanisms to constituents and so on. This makes it easier for NGOs to cross the boundary between civil and political society, direct and representative democracy, or 'voice and vote', in their international advocacy work, which is why there is so much discussion today about NGO legitimacy, accountability and representation.[21] So while the state is definitely 'out' of civil society and the non-partisan political activity of associations is definitely 'in', everything between these two extremes remains an object of dispute. The only acceptable compromise seems to be that political parties are *in* civil society when they out of office and *out* of civil society when they are in.

In case the situation is not sufficiently muddy, the boundary between civil society and the market is even less clear, especially in societies where market institutions are not well developed. Here again there is disagreement between those who fear for the purity of the civic spirit when contaminated by contact with business, and those like Ernest Gellner who argue that business – or at least the private-property relations and market institutions business needs to flourish – are inescapably a part of civil society. A strong tradition of civil society thinking (going back to John Locke) equates civil society with private economic activity, a tradition that is echoed today by the increasing use of non-profit agencies in the provision of social (and some economic) services, especially to low-income groups. Critics of this tradition see civil society as a political phenomenon, consigning service-providers to the not-for-profit sector of the marketplace and insisting on the independence of citizens' groups from all economic interests. Both Michael Walzer and Christopher Lasch insist that civil society is a sphere of life – a market-free zone – in which 'money is devalued', while Jean Cohen and Andrew Arato conclude that 'only a concept of civil society differentiated from the economy (and "bourgeois society") can become the center of a critical social and political theory in market economies.'[22] In practice, however, it is difficult to draw these distinctions in such a watertight manner. It was the market women of Sierra Leone, for example, who (acting collectively) thronged the streets of Freetown in 1996 and again in 1997 to ensure that democratic elections went ahead. Likewise, Ashutosh Varshney's research in India has shown that business associations that tie together the economic interests of Hindus and Muslims in Indian cities have been crucial in reducing the incidence of intercommunal violence (or exacerbating it where they are absent). And in Cuba, it is small-scale, informal enterprises that provide some space for independent organization where other forms of association are controlled by the state.[23]

This confusion is partly due to a failure to specify what kind of 'business' is being talked about. The institutional and legally mandated aims of a multinational corporation like Shell or IBM, for example, are different to those of sections of the business community that exist, at least in part, to generate a social good or advance a collective interest, such as cooperatives, credit unions, community enterprises and public–private partnerships with NGO participation, though in the age of the 'civil (that is, socially and environmentally responsible) corporation', maybe this judgement needs revising too.[24] In developing societies where the formal sector of the economy is often very small, most economic activity takes place in the informal sector anyway where social and market relations, business and civil society are inextricably interwoven. One also needs to distinguish between profit-seeking activities by individual enterprises and the civic or political role of business associations – like the Transatlantic Business Dialogue or a national chamber of commerce. Logically, the former would be excluded from civil society but the latter would not. Such associations could have an important role to play in encouraging attitudes of cooperation and trust, as well as representing the interests of their members.

The most difficult and contested question about 'who is in and who is out' revolves around the definition of 'civil' and 'uncivil' society, a debate explored in chapter 3 because it concerns the nature of the 'good society', the role of the family and much else besides, not simply the characteristics of associations. But it is worth mentioning that models of associational life find it difficult to exclude any non-state or non-market institution so long as they meet the structural or analytical criteria for membership described above. Of course, some writers do exclude associations of which they disapprove, but not on any grounds that can be defended without considerable intellectual gymnastics and the impo- sition of a particular – and therefore partial – definition of the good, the bad and the ugly. Would the Catholic Family and Human Rights Institute (an NGO that lobbied the United Nations to abandon the commitments on women's rights made at the Beijing Conference in 1995) be excluded by pro-choice groups, and vice versa?[25] Is the National Rifle Association legitimate, or not, and who decides? In my view, structural models of civil society hold water only if all non- coercive associations are allowed to be included, but even if one agrees on 'who is in and who is out', would these judge- ments hold true across different geographical and cultural contexts?

Associational life in cross-cultural perspective

'The same is never the same' is a watchword of feminism, and the same applies to voluntary associations. Civil society theory, for the most part, has been developed in Europe and the USA, and makes a series of assumptions about the rights and responsibilities of associations, the characteristics they should cultivate, and the roles they should play in society that may not travel well across countries, cultures and different periods in time. They may not even be accurate for different communities within the same country, like African-American associational life in America, for example, or Islamic voluntary associations in England. Yet a proper understanding of these traditions is essential if one holds to an associational view of civil society. Norms of participation are different among whites and African-Americans in the USA, for example, with the latter more likely to take part in protest and campaigning activities as part of an oppositional culture that characterizes many of their associations.[26] Islamic and Confucian cultures think differently about belonging, solidarity and citizenship, in part because of a stress on the collective rather than the individual. And in Africa, notions of the 'voluntary' are complicated by the continuing importance of identities that are inherited, not chosen.

For some, these are simple questions to answer: since civil society is the product of a specific period in the evolution of the West, it cannot exist, let alone prosper, in non-Western societies. For Ernest Gellner, John Hall and others, civil society and Islam are mutually exclusive alternatives because Islam as an institution cannot be left and entered freely. 'You can join the Labour Party without slaughtering a sheep', as Gellner famously remarked, 'and leave it without incurring the death penalty for apostasy'.[27] Times are changing, however, both for the Labour Party and for Islam. Recent Islamic scholars have shown that elements of voluntarism existed in traditional associations (such as guilds, trusts and foundations), just as new associations that would be clearly classified as voluntary in the West are beginning to emerge.[28] In Turkey, for example, independent associations of urban working women with freely chosen memberships coexist with Islamic associations that are closed to other faiths. There are certainly major problems in associational life in the Arab world – co-option by the state, for example, that makes it difficult for associations to promote accountability – but this is not because such functions are impossible to play by definition.

The same applies in Africa, where cultural and religious institutions expressing a collective identity based on clan or tribe coexist with newer, cross-ethnic forms of association that have emerged in response to urbanization, education and the development of the market economy, including churches, labour unions, farmers' organizations, human rights NGOs and the independent media. Academic battles still rage between those who claim that African societies are too fragmented along particularistic lines to support any notion of the public good, and those who argue that traditional associational life in Africa carries with it the seeds of a true civil society, but on the ground in Kenya, Nigeria, South Africa and elsewhere this argument is already being answered by societies that are developing a richer tapestry of associational life containing threads from both these traditions.[29] Associations based on primordial attachments are a natural consequence of the ways in which African societies have been structured in the past.

In China and other Confucian-based societies, social memberships – at least historically – are non-optional and priority is given to the needs of the 'social whole', so it is no surprise that associations have always found it difficult to exist outside of government control. However, the Chinese government is trying to balance the economic advantages that NGOs bring to poverty-alleviation programmes with the political costs of associational life elsewhere, and is allowing state-sponsored GONGOS (government-organized NGOs) like the All-China Women's Federation increasing room to manoeuvre inside official structures, a position that gives them unusual access and potential influence.[30] These tensions will grow as the non-profit sector in China evolves, as in other countries with a similar cultural heritage such as Taiwan. The reality of associational life in non-Western cultures, then, is one of 'mix and match'. That is why civil society watchers have so much interest in Israel, Turkey, China and Iran, where the combination of different associational cultures is particularly marked. Far from being a problem, the development of different varieties of civil society is a cause for celebration, because it means that the associations that emerge – hybrid, fluid and maybe surprising to commentators in the West – might be able to avoid some of the problems encountered by their Western counterparts, answering in the process the charge that they are simply pawns of foreign powers. However, even if one accepts that civil society exists in China, Africa and the Islamic world, are associations – as individual organizations – the correct unit of analysis to use?

Organizations and ecosystems

Neo-Tocquevillians often focus on non-profit organizations or the 'non-profit sector', which is a subset of associational life as a whole. More useful, in my view, is to take a systems view of associational life that looks at the different components of civil society and how they interact both with each other and with public and private institutions. Like a complex and fragile ecosystem, civil society gains strength when grassroots groups, non-profit intermediaries and membership associations are linked together in ways that promote collective goals, cross-society coalitions, mutual accountability and shared reflection. This is one generalization that does hold up across many different contexts: 'the landscape of the third sector is untidy but wonderfully exuberant . . . what counts is not the confusion but the profusion.'[31] This is because theories of associational life rest on the assumption that associations promote pluralism by enabling multiple interests to be represented, different functions to be performed and a range of capacities to be developed. No one set of organizations could hope to cover more than a small subsection of these roles, capacities and interests, so institutional pluralism *within* civil society is essential.

Drawing from social capital theory, this means a balance between 'bonding' (connections within groups), 'bridging' (connections across them) and 'linking' (connections between associations, government and the market). Bonding may accentuate inequalities since associations will be used to promote the interests only of the groups concerned, and can lead to gridlock in the system as a result of special-interest politics. Bridging should reduce them over time as people dissolve their differences in a sense of the wider common interest, and linking should help all groups to prosper by making the right connections with institutions that can offer them support, resources, opportunities and influence.[32] However, without the security provided by strong in-group ties, bridging may expose those on the margins to environments in which they cannot compete on equal terms, or benefit the few that can prosper at the expense of the many who are left behind.

Strongly bonded associations (like community organizations) are more effective when they link together vertically and horizontally to form cross-cutting networks and federations that can take the struggle to the next level, and alliances across the lines of class, race and religion that build from a strong grassroots base. ACORN, PICO and the Industrial Areas Foundation in the USA are good examples, as are the peasant federations studied by Tony Bebbington that connect small-producer groups together in Latin America.[33] But non-profit intermediaries or NGOs are also important, providing much of the 'connective tissue' of civil society by providing specialist support, capacity-building and advocacy services to broader networks and alliances. SPARC, an NGO in Mumbai, has developed a worldwide reputation for this kind of role in support of the Shack Dwellers International movement. Advocacy groups (often downgraded by neo-Tocquevillians on the grounds that they can be divisive) may be especially important.

When civil society networks join forces on a scale and over a time-span significant enough to force through more fundamental change, they can be classified as social movements.

Successful social movements (think civil rights in the USA, the movement of the landless in Brazil, and the environmental and women's movements worldwide) tend to have three things in common – a powerful idea, ideal or policy agenda; effective communications strategies to get these ideas into politics, government and the media; and a strong constituency or social base that provides the muscle required to make those targets listen and ensure that constituency views are accurately represented. When these three things come together, success is possible. In the USA, for example, the Living Wage Campaign has succeeded in getting legislation adopted in a number of states and cities despite a conservative Congress (including a 19 per cent pay rise for employees of municipal contractors in Chicago in 2002), while STISSS, the healthcare workers' union in El Salvador, has recently persuaded government to outlaw the privatization of healthcare because of its effects in excluding the poor.[34] Arguably, the most successful social movement in America over the last twenty years has been the rise of neo-conservatism, anchored in the associations of the religious right (like the 'Promise Keepers' and the 'Moral Majority'), but well connected both to think-tanks – like the Heritage Institute – and to the Republican Party.[35]

As in a real ecosystem, all parts need to be present and connected if the system is to operate effectively. Remove or weaken one part, or strengthen others artificially, and the system breaks down. An insufficient density, diversity or depth of associations leaves societies more vulnerable to authoritarian rule because the ecosystem cannot withstand external shocks. For example, if only one independent newspaper or watchdog organization exists, governments can easily throttle dissent (think of Zimbabwe under Robert Mugabe), but if thirty exist, at least some will survive (think of Kenya, Chile or even China). Worst of all is homogeneity, the Achilles heel of ecosystems both natural and social. Yet real associational ecosystems are replete with gaps, weaknesses and donor-led conformity. Labour unions in the USA today represent only one-third of the workers they represented fifty years ago.[36] Informal associations at the grassroots are often ignored or neglected, but they were vital to the struggle, for example, against apartheid in South Africa or for democracy in China today – like yard and street resident committees, burial and temple societies, farmers' associations and youth clubs. Theda Skocpol has made a special study of the decline of 'locally rooted but nationally active' cross-class membership associations in the USA like the American Legion and the AFL-CIO (the umbrella movement for the US labour movement), arguing that US civil society has moved 'from membership to management' over the last forty years.[37] Progressive social movements are weak in the USA, even with its strong tradition of associational life. This is partly because the liberal establishment tends to be divorced from grassroots activism, just as grassroots activists tend to be weakly linked to the centres of power in Washington DC.

If concentrated power is bad for democracy in general, it is difficult to argue that it is good for civil society, yet some of the trends in associational life over the past decade have come dangerously close to this effect. There has been a worldwide professionalization of the non-profit sector and a gradual distancing of associations from their social base – in part the result of foreign aid and government funding that is driven by strong neo-Tocquevillian tendencies among donors. Funds have gone overwhelmingly to NGOs in capital cities, while Northern NGOs have dominated the emergence of transnational advocacy networks. This is not strengthening civil society, but promoting certain associations over others on the basis of preconceived notions of what civil society should look like. Even if one rejects the thesis that civil society is in decline, it is impossible to ignore the fact that its shape is changing in important ways in every part of the world. This is to be expected, since associational life is never static, but even if the associational ecosystem maintains its health and strength while its shape is changing, does it follow that this will have predictable effects?

Forms and norms

The claim that economic and political success is directly related to the strength and health of associational life is common to neo-Toquevillian thinking, especially the work of Robert Putnam, based first on his comparison between northern and southern Italy and more recently on his monumental surveys of 'social capital' in the USA. In Putnam's view, associations breed social capital and social capital breeds success – the 'forms' of associational life produce the 'norms' of the good society. Putnam's work has since spawned a thriving debate, but if everything related in this chapter is true – that the depth of the 'associational revolution' may have been exaggerated; that fundamental uncertainties remain about the boundaries of civil society, political society and the market; that associational life varies greatly across context and culture; that associational ecosystems are full of gaps and disconnections; and that civil societies are always 'works in progress' – then it stands to reason that the link between forms and norms will be complex, contingent and contested. A strong civil society, as noted in chapter 1, would not necessarily make society strong and civil. Why not?

3
Civil Society as the Good Society

When the Egyptian scholar–activist Saad Eddin Ibrahim stood up to defend himself in front of the Supreme State Security Court in Cairo one July day in 2002, he focused on one key phrase, 'civil society',[1] by which he meant a society where all could be free to speak their minds and have their voices heard. Although accused on spurious grounds of financial mismanagement as the head of a prominent Egyptian NGO, the Ibn Khaldoun Centre, Ibrahim was arrested because he – and by extension 'civil society' – was perceived to pose a threat to the reigning political order. Not many of us would be as brave or principled as this, but all of us carry in our hearts and minds a vision of the world as we would want it to be – ruled, at the most general level, by love and forgiveness, truth and beauty, courage and compassion. Even in an age obsessed by terrorism, mercifully few people wake up each morning to plan the final details of an attack on the World Trade Centre or the Federal Building in Oklahoma City, select their targets for a killing spree at the local high school, or identify which of their opponents are next in line for ethnic cleansing. Of course, the details of the good society are subject to a never-ending debate about ends and means, necessary compromises and trade-offs between different interests and objectives, but the idea of the good society remains a driving force behind the best of contemporary politics and collective action. Increasingly, 'civil society' is used as shorthand for the kind of society in which we want to live. The use of civil society as a metaphor for the good society has its roots in the Greek *polis* and the 'commonwealths' described in chapter 1, in religious doctrines about spiritual communities such as the Islamic *Ummah* or the Jewish *Tikkun Olam*, and in Kantian thinking about a global ethical community or the *civitas humana* of William Roepke and other conservatives.[2] In its now-dominant liberal-democratic form it was the inspiration for dissident groups in eastern Europe and the former Soviet Union during the 1980s, where it symbolized a call to 'institutionalize the principles of citizenship on which modern liberal, democratic politics are based' and became almost a synonym – or 'shining emblem' – for democracy and freedom – and even for 'decency' in general.[3] For Vaclav Havel, 'civic society' was 'the social order towards which all modern democratic societies are gradually working', while Victor Perez-Diaz has made a similar argument for the 'return of civil society' in Spain after the end of General Franco's regime.[4] Since 1989 these ideas have been detached somewhat from their liberal-democratic moorings, and taken up by a wider range of ideological and cultural positions including the global justice movement on the left (mobilized at the World Social Forum each year under the slogan 'another world is possible'), scholars arguing against self-interest as the basis for social science and public policy, feminists searching for a rationality not based on 'economic man', opposition movements in Kenya, Zambia and many other developing countries, and critics in non-Western settings who see in Islamic 'civil society' the roots of a 'civilized life' that is different from the West.

Not all of these positions use the precise phrase 'civil society', but they do share an image of civil society as a desirable social order or self-image of modernity defined in normative terms. Although these norms sometimes differ, tolerance, non-discrimination, non-violence, trust and cooperation are common denominators, along with freedom and democracy so long as these are not defined exclusively in Western terms – freedom from want being as important as freedom from arbitrary government intervention, and democracy being valued in the marketplace and global governance as well as in domestic politics. In this sense, civil society represents the institutionalization of 'civility' as a different way of being and living in the world, or a different kind of society in which all institutions operate in ways that reinforce these positive social norms – in short, 'a society that is civil'.

At the transnational level, these ideas are reflected in the rising popularity of 'global civil society', not as the additional layer of associational life described in chapter 2, but as a mechanism by which new global norms are developed and cemented around notions of universal human rights, international cooperation and the peaceful resolution of differences in the global arena. George Soros's 'global open society', Richard Falk's 'humane governance', David Held's 'cosmopolitan democracy', the 'global civil society' of John Keane and Mary Kaldor, my own 'future positive', and the 'global ethical community' of even a philosopher as gloomy as Peter Singer all represent versions of this same idea, despite the fact that we are at least a generation away from any kind of cosmopolitan democracy or 'cosmocracy'.

There is, however, an important difference between 'a society that is civil' because it possesses high levels of generalized trust and cooperation (or 'social capital' to use a now-conventional shorthand), and one that is 'civil' because it succeeds in solving particular public-policy dilemmas in ways that are just and effective. Some civil society enthusiasts (especially the neo-Toquevillians) might argue that these two understandings are the same, since such generalized norms – anchored in a healthy associational life – will facilitate effective public-policy making as people of goodwill come to a sensible and fair consensus over matters of pressing concern. But in the analysis that follows it is important to keep them separate, for two interrelated reasons. First, because the correlation between associational life and the generation of generalized trust and cooperation is often weaker than supposed, and second, because progress towards just and effective policy outcomes is usually associated with action across different sets of institutions – government and business as well as voluntary associations.

The achievement of the good society requires both norms of behaviour that infuse institutions with values-based energy and direction, and political settlements that legitimize and sustain these values and directions in the polity. Working alone, voluntary associations can secure neither of these things, since norms and values are fostered in families, schools and workplaces as well as in associations, and political and legal ordering by government is required to secure all social contracts. In recent history, a rich associational life has been only weakly correlated with the eradication of poverty and the achievement of other national development goals in 'high performers' like South Korea, Botswana and Chile, though, as chapter 1 pointed out, it has never been irrelevant. A strong, purposeful state has been as or more influential. Naturally, when development requires the overthrow and reconstruction of state institutions (as in eastern Europe or South Africa), major social transformations do tend to be led by citizens and their associations, but in general, nation building, not civil society building, is the core task of development in its early stages. Some societies (like China) are making progress with a weak associational life, at least defined in Western terms, while others (like the USA) have strong third sectors but continuing problems of inequality and discrimination. Americans gave more to charity in 2001 than ever before ($212 billion to be exact) but America is no nearer to solving its pressing social problems than before.[5] Given these varying experiences, how is 'a civil society' to be created?

Associational life and the good society

We saw in chapter 2 how structural and normative understandings of civil society became conflated through the experience of civic and political movements like Solidarity in Poland and – on the other side of the Atlantic – through the arguments of neo-Toquevillians who saw voluntary associations as the 'gene-carriers' of the good society. If the good society is defined as one where free associations flourish, then the tendency to conflate these understandings is even stronger. The 'demand for a return to civil society', as Daniel Bell has written, 'is the demand for a return to a manageable scale of social life . . . which emphasizes voluntary associations . . . arguing that decisions should be made locally and should not be controlled by the state and its bureaucracies'.[6] However, there are good reasons to doubt the link between ends and means that is implied in this statement, since in Michael Walzer's oft-quoted words, 'the associational life of civil society is the ground where all visions of the good are worked out and tested, *and* proved to be partial, incomplete and ultimately unsatisfying. . . . there is no possibility of choosing, like the old anarchists, civil society alone'. Why not?

In Norman Rockwell's famous painting 'Freedom of Speech', the humble citizen stands tall, shining with integrity, to speak his mind at the local town-hall meeting. In the Rockwell school of civil society thinking, communities, citizens and associations are nearly always upright, honest and noble, but in the real world they are nearly always mixed in their motivations and their interests. This constitutes a difficult problem for the 'civil society revivalists' as they have been called, since those in this school of thought insist that voluntary social interaction produces high and generalized levels of trust and cooperation, which in turn are essential for democracy and social progress.[7] Their key hypothesis is that communities, networks and associations are 'microclimates' in which skills are learned, values and loyalties developed, and caring and cooperation – instead of competition and violence – become the rational ways to behave, and there are three reasons why this should be true. First, the level and frequency of face-to-face interaction that is possible in associations or small communities means that incentives for trusting and cooperative behaviour are likely to be stronger: as a member of a small group, I can see or judge the consequences of my uncooperative actions and reap the rewards of cooperation from each of my colleagues – 'you scratch my back and I'll scratch yours, or we both scratch out each other's eyes'. Secondly, social norms are likely to be reinforced through familiarity and peer pressure, since either I agree to play by the rules or I join someone else's club. Third, the members of a group can see on a small scale that the welfare of the whole depends on the individual actions of its members, thereby anchoring the kinds of behaviour that are essential if democracy is to function in the public interest at higher levels too.

The next step in the 'revivalist' argument is to demonstrate that these generalized norms feed through into the effective functioning of democracy, and from there to the realization of the good society since a functioning democracy should produce a social consensus on political goals. Nancy Rosenblum lists the 'key virtues for democracy' as follows: 'civility, or treating people identically and with easy spontaneity, and fairness, or speaking out against arbitrary injustice'.[8] Whether membership in voluntary associations actually generates these virtues is debatable, but a link could certainly be made in theory since regular interaction with groups of overlapping memberships should strengthen 'civility' while incentives to cooperation should strengthen 'fairness'.

So far so good, until the genie of difference is introduced into the equation. Early in the work that eventually led to *Bowling Alone*, Robert Putnam's blockbuster about the 'collapse and revival of American community', a seminar was held at the Harvard Divinity School to discuss the subject of social capital. Putnam, as expected, extolled the virtues of choirs, choral societies and other voluntary associations, until one member of the audience piped up with the following question: 'But Bob, what is the choir *singing*?'[9] As this question implies, associational life per se is unlikely to guarantee a particular set of social norms and values, still less the connection between these norms and the goals of the good society, whenever associations and their members vary widely in their characteristics, purposes and beliefs. 'The rebirth of civil society is always riddled with dangers since it gives freedom to despots and democrats alike.'[10]

The reality is that norms vary between different associations in the same society or culture and between different cultures and societies – not exactly rocket science, but crucial to a clear view of potential pathways to social progress. Notions of reciprocity, for example, are not the same in white America, African-American communities in the USA, tribal societies in Africa, religious communities such as Islam and Judaism, and villages in China. Some norms – like trust and even cooperation – have a different value for people in different circumstances. Neither is an unalloyed or general 'good' since one person's confidence may be abused by less scrupulous others, especially in societies shot through by inequality, corruption and exploitation – think of landlords in rural India for example, governments who lie to their citizens, or the directors of fallen giant Enron who were indicted in 2002. Generally, poor people do best when they are cautious reciprocators, that is, predisposed to cooperate but unafraid to retaliate when others take advantage of them. To be uncritically trusting when power is unequally distributed and information is imperfect is a dangerous strategy for social advancement, so it is misleading to aggregate these norms at the level of communities, associations or societies as a whole. Both trust and mistrust must be discriminating.

Even if the same norms were universally interpreted to mean the same thing and weighted with the same importance, they might be put to different uses at the next level of specificity in defining the good society's ends and means. For example, people might develop high levels of trust for each other but lose it in the institutions – like government and the market – that are vital for promoting social goals. So voting may decline even as volunteering increases (exactly the correlation that has been observed for contemporary America, where associational life is in danger of becoming a substitute for politics).[11] Cooperation may be expressed in actions that are socially inclusive or exclusive, for or against affirmative action, tolerant of economic inequality or not. Different norms might even cancel each other out, like volunteering for the Ku Klux Klan, which does nothing for fairness but might still strengthen cooperation, at least with other members. The 'greatest' or 'long civic generation' that is praised by the revivalists for its vitality after the Second World War was also the generation in which the lynching of African-Americans reached its peak, Japanese-Americans were interned while their property was sold for a pittance, and racial discrimination in jobs, industry, education and voting became routine.[12] In any case, the principal ingredient in volunteering is enthusiasm, not necessarily an activism driven by a particular social vision. Voluntary associations are arenas for personal ambition and power as well as for sacrifice and service. 'Pillar of the community, soccer coach, wife beater' as a sign on the New York subway reads. As in the case of the choir, the good society depends on what volunteers do and why they do it, not simply who they are.

Most important of all, norms and values do vary considerably between associations. At some point in civil society discussion, one bright spark will come up with the obvious question about the Mafia. 'Is the Mafia a member?' they will ask, expecting the whole of civil society theory to come crashing down like a house of cards when they hear the answer 'no'. Since 11 September 2001 the disproving example of choice has been al-Qaeda, and no doubt another is waiting in the wings. But extreme examples like this can be dismissed as violent criminals, just as similar elements would be dismissed if they were criminals in government or criminals in business. Other cases are more significant, like Lebanon (during that country's long civil war) and Rwanda (prior to the genocide in 1994) where strong networks of voluntary associations did foment inter-group violence. Rwanda had the highest density of associations in sub-Saharan Africa, while the 'vast majority' of associations in Lebanon during the 1970s and 1980s were 'exclusionary, divisive' and constantly at war with each other.[13] In both cases, associations were organized along ethnic or religious lines and mobilized politically, which at least in some eyes disqualifies them from civil society membership. In translation, Interahamwe, the name given to the Hutu killing-machine in Rwanda, means 'those who attack together', a chilling echo of the fact that Timothy McVeigh and his fellow Oklahoma City bombers were members of bowling leagues in the USA, and that the students responsible for the Columbine High School massacre a year later reputedly spent their morning by bowling with their classmates.[14] *Pace* Putnam, if killing, as among the Interahamwe, is a 'civic duty', then better 'bowling alone than conspiring together'.[15] Clearly, the problem here is not collective action per se, but collective action allied to other factors that turn it in particular directions for good or for ill. But if this is the case, then the argument must hold for both the positive cases and the negative – meaning that generalized notions of associational life and its effects are unlikely to be tenable.

In any case, the most significant problems for civil society revivalists do not emerge from the extreme clashes of values that characterize the behaviour of terrorists like McVeigh and Osama bin Laden or the killers of civilians in zones of civil war, but from the ambiguous moral effects of ordinary, non-violent associations with different views, purposes and characteristics – the inevitable result, of course, of the pluralism that civil society is supposed to protect. After all, civil society is known as the realm of 'particularity' – the place where, whoever we are, we can find a home without asking for permission from above. This is why attempts to define the problem of 'uncivil' society away inevitably founder in the grey waters of associational life, especially when allied to the whiff of authoritarian moralizing that often accompanies judgements about 'who is in and who is out', and a tendency to romanticize the past in order to justify a return to ideologically driven 'realities' in the present. Some associations could be universally excluded because they deliberately seek to destroy through violence the rights of others to participate, but judgements about the rest would be unlikely to meet a universal consensus. And although there is some evidence that positive norms and values feed through into high levels of performance among associations providing services to the poor or advocating on their behalf, there is no evidence that this is generally true in comparison to institutions doing similar things in the public and private sectors. Rather, the factors underlying outstanding performance seem to cut across these different institutions – high levels of accountability, for example, a clear focus, good listening skills, and the minimum degree of hierarchy required to make decisions. This is especially true for the supposed superiority of faith-based associations in America, which is not a surprising conclusion to anyone who has experienced incompetence from charities as well as businesses or governments, but may be discomfiting for those who wish to privilege one sector over others on ideological grounds.

Given these high levels of difference and diversity, it is not surprising that the moral reality of associational life doesn't necessarily add up at the macro level. Conditions in the Weimar Republic during the rise of Adolf Hitler are often cited to support this point – a dense network of citizens' groups unable or unwilling to counter the increasing power of the Nazi Party. Similar claims have been made about Italy under Fascism (where the choirs that Putnam claims sustained Italian democracy sang Mussolini's tunes) and civil society in the Balkans after the death of Marshall Tito.[16] However, one doesn't have to look back in time for useful illustrations, since associational life in the aggregate is never uniform in its effects. Religious organizations are especially interesting in this respect, since they are home to both liberal and conservative elements, inclusionary and exclusionary norms of behaviour, openness and prejudice. The hardline Protestant evangelicals of the Church Society in the UK or REFORM (formed in part to oppose the ordination of women), have a very different normative agenda to the Methodists, Quakers, or Church of England, especially under Archbishop Rowan Williams. In the late 1980s, an unholy alliance between the Bulgarian orthodox church and chauvinist elements in politics fought to preserve 'new forms of backwardness' as the country opened to the West (mirroring the emergence of Hindu nationalism in India), while right-wing populism in America has had gay and reproductive rights in its sights for a generation or more.[17] Are these examples of uncivil society, or merely illustrations of associations with different views on the 'restless battlefield of interests'?[18] The existence of diversity inevitably complicates the link between forms and norms that lies at the heart of neo-Toquevillian thinking. Adam Seligman captures this dilemma well: 'when associations are ethically construed as different normative universes, they represent not the realization but the destruction of civil life . . . on the other hand, when they are built around the principle of interest they cannot mediate or mitigate interest-motivated action in the name of some higher ethical unity'.[19]

Inequality poses a particular problem for civil society theory since it invests associations and their members with different levels of social resources that we know from experience are used for individual advancement, not just the common interest. The biases introduced by education and income are especially pronounced in civic and political activity (the richer and more educated you are, the more likely you are to vote, make campaign contributions and participate in most classes of associations, at least in America). So 'although the decline of civic engagement is contentious, the inequality of civic engagement is unambiguous'.[20] Large differentials in the power of associations to make their voices heard, advance their agendas and consolidate their own interpretation of shared norms in the public sphere, are the enemy of the good society, and of democracy. That is why reducing inequality is a crucial part of any solution to the civil society puzzle. Even more destructive is discrimination based on race, caste, gender or sexual orientation, which is why some NGOs in India use the concept of 'twice-born civil society' to underline the importance of eradicating such divisions before society can be civil. The fact that associational life is home to racism, sexism, homophobia and small-scale violence (if we agree that only states – not civil societies –

go to war) is distressing to civil society revivalists, but it must be faced if we are to identify the steps that can be taken to render associational life an effective vehicle for realizing social goals.

Recognition of these inequalities provides a clue to the final reason why associational life is always incomplete as a path to the good society. By themselves, voluntary associations cannot aggregate their interests in order to secure the political settlements that are crucial to development above the local level. This is especially true when strong but divided associations push against a weak state – as in the special-interest politics of the USA, inter-religious conflicts in the Lebanese civil war, or the 'anti-globalization' protests of Seattle and beyond (since no global government exists). Empirically this is not completely true, since shared interpretations of norms may develop among associations even if they are put to different uses, and high levels of self-organization and democratic representation can develop among likeminded sections of civil society, at least at certain times – when the interests of all associations in a country are threatened by a government, for example, or when associations come together to present a united political front during times of democratic transition (the Philippines under Ferdinand Marcos comes to mind as an example). In general, however, associational life has to be politically ordered if the huge diversity of positions and interests is to be consolidated in service to some broader national or international agenda.

These observations do not mean that no connection exists between associational life, the cultivation of positive social norms, and the aims of the good society, and in chapter 5 we will look at these connections in some detail. At their best, NGOs and other civic groups are characterized by attitudes of service and solidarity, beyond the particularities of special-interest lobbying or identity politics. But such connections are always ambiguous. To say that a civil society 'requires' trust and mutuality is true, but associational life doesn't generate these things by itself, especially in deeply fractured societies. Visions of the good society that rest on voluntary action will always be built, if not on shifting sands then certainly on shaky foundations.

States, markets, and societies that are civil

If a strong civil society cannot create a society that is strong and civil, what can? The answer lies through action across different institutions directed at particular social goals. While governments, firms and families are not part of associational life as defined in chapter 2, they must be part of building a society that is civil because they influence both social norms and the political settlements that translate them into public policy. As Jean Cohen puts it, 'the problems facing US civil society are not due to moral decline but to the capture of politics and economics by special interests that block necessary reforms'.[21] So instead of fixating on one sector to the exclusion of the others (whether market, state or voluntary), we should look for institutional arrangements across society that secure whatever reforms are needed. In the good society, success, like failure, is always collective, especially at a time of civil corporations, uncivil society and network states.

This process has to start by recognizing – as did Gramsci – that the family is central to shaping the values, norms and dispositions of individuals. It may be somewhat romantic to claim, as does Stephen Carter, that 'the family is a place where we die to the Self', but it is surely correct to say, at the deepest level, that families are or should be the first 'civil societies', marked by sacrifice and caring for the other.[22] Trust, cooperation and other more specific political attitudes all begin to be formed in family relationships. Family life (along with schooling and work) takes up far more of most people's time than associational life, so it can be expected to influence their commitments especially strongly. Unlike trust, love and compassion are more likely to be unambiguously positive in their effects, not because they resolve higher-order social and political questions but because they create a foundation for radically different modes of behaviour on which new solutions can be built. Defined by the wonderfully named 'Institute for Research on Unlimited Love' at Case Western University, 'the essence of love is to affectively affirm as well as unselfishly delight in the well being of others, and to engage in acts of care and service on their behalf, without exception, in an enduring and constant way'. Not a bad foundation for the good society, it seems to me, so the formation and nurturing of loving and supportive family relationships – in which both employers and governments obviously play a role – is crucial to building a society that is civil.

The role of business in creating the good society is a deeply contentious issue in contemporary politics, but inescapable because no modern society can pursue progressive social goals without access to the surplus that market economies create. On the other hand, economic actors can only operate effectively if they are embedded in a wider civil society that harbours social interaction based on trust, honesty and non-violence, even though real existing capitalism tends to destroy these things over time. In other words, a civil society cannot survive where there are no markets, and markets need a civil society to prosper. In an age of 'socially responsible capitalism' one would expect these 'zero-sum' relationships to be replaced, or at least mitigated, by corporations that hold themselves accountable to the 'triple bottom line', using their economic activities to raise minimum wage and labour standards and enable their employees to take a full part in associational life by providing adequate childcare and flexible working arrangements. The further business moves in this direction, the greater its contribution will be to creating a society that is civil.

However, even loving families and socially responsible capitalism will create – or fail to redress – inequalities of power, access and opportunity. Dealing explicitly with these inequalities is a precondition for societies that are civil, and this task must include government action to 'level the playing field', legislate against discrimination, change the 'rules of the game', protect labour and other standards, guarantee adequate social security and childcare arrangements, and do all the other things that associational life, firms and families can't or won't do for themselves. America's unwillingness to accept this fact drives her desire to seek solutions to structural problems through voluntary action, a journey that is destined to end in tears. For example, women may gain more access to employment through the marketplace or non-profit support programmes, but they still need legislation on equal pay and childcare provision in order to take advantage of these opportunities. The disconnection that poor people typically feel is as much from the structures of power (economic and political) as from each other, so a strong, democratically accountable state is just as important as associational life to the eradication of poverty. Even Alexis de Tocqueville acknowledged that 'if men are to remain civilized or to become so, the art of associating together must grow and improve in the same ratio in which the equality of conditions is increased'. 'Good neighbors cannot replace good government.'[23]

This is a difficult message to communicate, however, to some neo-Tocquevillians who still see government as a bugbear despite the role of the state in securing the preconditions for equal civic participation and legal protection for associations. For them, it is moral values that have collapsed since 1945, not the support structures that enable still-moral beings to fulfil their potential as citizens, carers, parents and volunteers, as well as workers and consumers. There is a clear fault-line here between those who see associational life as irredeemably particular (requiring government intervention to enforce universal norms, rights and standards), and those who see a negotiated consensus in civil society as the only contract that will last. There is a similar and parallel divide between those who claim that social mores are structured by politics, and those who claim that politics are structured by social mores. Seeing 'government as the domain of common purpose and identity', and civil society as the realm of 'anarchy, private oppression, and the private engrossment of collective resources' may seem fanciful at a time when private interests seem to have more influence over government than ever, but since states retain a monopoly over the means of violence and coercion, it is difficult to see how any other set of institutions can act as guarantors of equal treatment in this way.[24] Zygmunt Bauman argues that 'zones of civility' in everyday life are *only* possible if the means of institutional violence are stored elsewhere. In this sense it would be disastrous if we were to 'give up on the state's ability to establish the rule of law or democracy through elections and legislatures, and instead give civic associations – the political equivalent of the private sector – a chance to do their thing'.[25]

In any case, major social transformations or systemic changes in politics and economics have rarely been achieved by associations acting alone, even when channelled through broad-based social movements. Achieving these things requires a series of reforms across society so that states, markets and intermediary associations harness their different energies to some common purpose – as countries in east Asia did from the 1950s to the 1980s, or successful states in India like Kerala and West Bengal. In Kerala, this took the form of agreements between a democratic government and a powerful labour movement that resulted in social and economic gains far more impressive than in other Indian states.[26] In Taiwan and South Korea, a less democratic state and a weaker set of intermediary associations still developed sufficient synergy to transform the structure of production at rates unknown in history, though of course there were many other factors in play that had little to do with state–society relations. These episodes of constructive engagement have all been based on social contracts between government, business and civil society that secure and maintain a minimum level of consensus around the trade-offs that characterize the process of development – growth and redistribution, short-term sacrifices and long-term benefits, private, public and collective interests. What is the key to successful development? 'It's the polity, stupid' – not 'generalized trust' but social, economic and political energy strategically directed at the specifics of each set of challenges through coordinated action across different sets of institutions. This is the path to the good society.

Conclusion

As this brief excursion through theory has shown, the connections between a strong civil society (measured by a healthy associational ecosystem) and a society that is strong and civil (defined as one considered 'good' by the majority of its citizens) are complex and contingent – no surprise there then. However, one conclusion is clear: those who search for the good society must find their allies – and identify their enemies – wherever they can, among those elements of government, business and associational life which share a similar agenda, since not all do. However, if the good society requires coordinated action between different institutions all pulling in the same direction, how do societies decide in which direction to go, and whether it is the right one as conditions and circumstances continue to change over time? How are choices made, trade-offs negotiated, and ends reconciled with means in ways that are just and effective? For answers to these questions, we must turn to the theory of the public sphere.

4
Civil Society as the Public Sphere

In nineteenth-century Bengal, a long-forgotten but once celebrated exchange took place between Rabindranath Tagore and Nabinchandra Sen.[1] The subject of debate between the famous poet and his less famous but equally erudite opponent was the appropriateness of public mourning, a concept very different to the private grief of traditional Hindu teaching and – according to Sen – very much an invention of India's colonial masters, the British. Tagore's position revolved around the necessary development of a new kind of sensibility that accepted the responsibility to mourn the deaths of those who had devoted their lives to public service, or the struggle for independence, 'politically' – that is, in full view and as part of a strategy to consolidate new norms and alliances across old and familiar boundaries. Without such a public sensibility, progress would be much more difficult to achieve because pre-existing divisions and the primacy of different lives lived in private would make it impossible to solidify a united front in favour of reform. 'Publics are formed when we turn from our separate affairs to face common problems, and face each other in dialogue and discussion.'[2]

The concept of a 'public' – a whole polity that cares about the common good and has the capacity to deliberate about it democratically – is central to civil society thinking. The development of shared interests, a willingness to cede some territory to others, the ability to see something of oneself in those who are different and work together more effectively as a result – all these are crucial attributes for effective governance, practical problem-solving, and the peaceful resolution of our differences. In its role as the 'public sphere', civil society becomes the arena for argument and deliberation as well as for association and institutional collaboration: a 'non-legislative, extra-judicial, public space in which societal differences, social problems, public policy, government action and matters of community and cultural identity are developed and debated'.[3] The extent to which such spaces thrive is crucial to the health of a democracy, since if only certain truths are represented, if alternative viewpoints are silenced by exclusion or suppression, and if one set of voices is heard more loudly than those of others (those of the wealthy, for example, or of a particular ideological orientation), then the 'public' interest suffers. A good example would be the debate over genetically modified foods, an issue that arouses strong views on all sides and whose outcome will be crucial to the health and welfare of millions of people as consumers and producers all across the world. In these circumstances, an objective reading of the options and the evidence is crucial to coming to some legitimate resolution, but this is precisely what is lacking from the current mix of corporate lobbying, sensational media coverage of 'Frankenstein foods', and blanket condemnation by the anti-globalization protest movement. Against this background, the measures taken in 2002 by the British government – stimulating a broader debate through one-day summits, information films and public meetings – are to be welcomed, insufficient as they are, but such measures would be vital for any question on which views diverge and no immediate consensus is likely – the pros and cons of stem cell research, for example, war against Iraq, or the curtailment of civil liberties in the 'war against terrorism'. Is it the duty of the citizen to spy on their neighbours or defend them from incursions against their privacy? Only broad-based debate can define the public interest, not dictats by government. Such debates are the very stuff of a democracy.

Ideas about the public sphere stretch back at least to Aristotle, for whom a disposition to seek each other's company and form 'political friendships' in search of the common good was characteristic of all good citizens. Since only certain people qualified as citizens in ancient Greece this was not a particularly 'public' public, and later theories of the public sphere addressed this problem by stressing the power relations that permeate communications and the virtues of inclusive conversation. John Keane traces the history of ideas about the public sphere in three different phases: as a weapon against despots in eighteenth-century Europe and North America; as a means, throughout the twentieth century, to critique the increasing commodification of areas of life thought to be free from the influence of the market; and later still, as a contemporary defence of public service broadcasting in service to democracy.[4]

We saw in chapter 1 how a strong tradition of thinking in Keane's first and second phases grew up in the USA, where it was rooted in the Founding Fathers' belief in a system of government in which opinions would be refined through public debate and practical compromise. This system was undermined from the very beginning by inequalities of voice and vote based around discrimination, and by the gradual commercialization of the means of communication through which publics formed and engaged with each other beyond the traditional face-to-face interactions that characterized small, homogeneous communities. It was these concerns that led later writers in America – like John Dewey, Hannah Arendt and Richard Sennett – to lament the decline of the public sphere as a result of increasing self-absorption and the commercial colonization of the media, a tradition that continues in the USA today through the work of Harry Boyte, Sara Evans and others like the Kettering Foundation who see civil society as an autonomous space for generating democratic ideas and innovations.

By common consent, however, the most successful attempt to elaborate these ideas came from Jurgen Habermas, who theorized in highly elaborate terms the existence of a 'discursive public sphere' that enabled citizens to talk about common concerns in conditions of freedom, equality and non-violent interaction – a body of thought summarized under the umbrella of 'critical theory'. These qualifying conditions are crucial, because they establish a boundary within which conversations must take place if they are to qualify as democratic, and therefore effective in generating the outcomes the public sphere is supposed to produce. A public sphere, says Keane, 'is a particular type of spatial relationship between two or more people . . . connected by means of communication . . . in which non-violent controversies erupt . . . concerning the power relations operating within their given milieu of interaction'.[5] Early examples included the coffee houses of eighteenth-century London and Edinburgh, the fabled town-hall meetings of revolutionary New England, and the debates that animated the public squares of all historic cities. Contemporary examples range from the 'micro' public spheres of literary circles and book clubs, citizens' juries and 'deliberation days', through public radio and television, independent newspapers, facilitated debates, referenda and deliberative opinion polls at the national level, to potentially global public spheres like the World Social Forum or public-access Internet sites such as that of opendemocracy, which bills itself as an arena for intelligent conversation in cyberspace between people of different and dissenting views.[6] All societies possess a range of these public spheres at different levels, which rise and fall according to the issues at hand and the circumstances of the moment. A single, unified public sphere would be impossible at any significant scale, but regardless of their level or size, what takes place inside them?

In Habermas's thinking, participants in public conversations will come to a consensus about the great issues of the day through the force of rational argument. It is the best ideas that will triumph, not the loudest voice – a somewhat quaint conclusion given the inequalities that characterize all contemporary societies. Critical theorists who follow Habermas lay great stress on the ethics and structures of these discourses, since unless they are carefully ordered there is no possibility that the public sphere can work as theory predicts. Habermas's ideas have also been criticized as ethnocentric, based as they are on a particular reading of 'rationality' that is rooted in the linear thinking of the Enlightenment. Nevertheless, the conviction that groups of people can change their minds by engaging with each other non-violently is critical to democracy, both because it makes political consensus possible and because it tends to mitigate extremist views on all sides of the political spectrum. Like rocks in a stream, the sharpness of different perspectives can be softened over time as they knock against each other.

Theories of the public sphere provide a powerful framework for interpreting the role played by civil society in social change, though their implications are often ignored by the neo-Tocquevillians or reduced by donor agencies to preserving the institutions of the independent media and building the communications capacities of NGOs. A functioning public sphere does rest on elements of the first two definitions of civil society explored in chapters 2 and 3 – a healthy associational ecosystem and action across institutions in search of the good society – but it is much more than the sum of these parts. Inclusive and objective public deliberation is feasible only through channels that are not completely captured by states or markets, so the condition of associational life and the regulatory frameworks imposed by government are always important factors. On the other hand, what takes place in the public sphere is, or is assumed to be, marked out by the normative values of the good society like tolerance for dissent, a willingness to argue without quitting the debate when other, more persuasive, voices take the stage, and a commitment to 'truth telling' in the traditions of the US civil rights movement. These norms are crucial if problems are genuinely to be resolved in the public interest, since there is no other way the public interest can be defined.

However, the public sphere is more than a combination of 'forms' and 'norms', because it is explicitly concerned with fashioning a democratic framework for the development and expression of collective visions about the basic 'rules of the game' – the judgements, priorities and trade-offs that guide the evolution of all successful societies. Theories of the public sphere demand a return to the practice of politics, not as an elite occupation in which the public takes part once every four or five years through elections, but as an ongoing process through which 'active citizens' can help to shape both the ends and means of the good society. The theory of the public sphere, consciously or not, is the basis for the current and widespread revival of interest in direct, deliberative or participatory democracy, or 'dialogic politics', as an essential complement to the representative components of political systems in contexts as diverse as Scottish devolution, village India, and the poverty reduction strategy papers promulgated by the World Bank. In this sense, civil society – as a set of capacities – and politics – as a set of processes – become united in the public sphere, providing an essential antidote to the depoliticization and fatalism that is so marked in contemporary Western societies.

Why is the public sphere important?

Dialogic politics offer a route – and perhaps the only route – to reach a legitimate normative consensus around a plurality of interests and positions assuming certain conditions are met – equality of voice and access, in particular, and a minimum of censorship so that the relevant information is available to all. Politics cannot be just unless the full range of views and interests is represented in a process in which all the protagonists agree to collaborate towards a resolution. At the very least, conversations in the public sphere can provide a reasoned justification for majority decisions, so helping to avoid the 'tyranny' of a weakly elected government. This was something that had concerned much earlier theorists of democracy like John Stuart Mill, who warned that the secret ballot would encourage voters to 'choose the politicians who most pandered to their interests rather than voting for the public good'.[7] The public sphere, by contrast, is centrally concerned with the processes of opinion and will formation that precede or surround the act of voting.

For Habermas, all modern states face a crisis of legitimacy that is rooted in the commodification of the public sphere, a process, he argues, that prevents publics from shaping state policy. Instead, they are manipulated by it. While the depth of this 'crisis' can be contested, it is clear that major social change can only come about when sufficient public debate has sorted through the issues and a community emerges to support it. Amitai Etzioni uses the example of action against smoking, which arrived after thirty years of public discussion, to illustrate this point.[8] The emergence of corporate social responsibility, widespread public debate about the legitimacy of war against Iraq, and rising concerns about globalization are other examples of the same process at work today. As in these cases, or with any of the compromises highlighted at the end of chapter 3, the common interest can only be found through democratic struggle and debate – we cannot find it unless we look for it together. Solutions are more likely to hold when all social groups have a say in the answers and a stake in their outcomes. We may never share a common vision of ends and means in the good society, but we can all be committed to a process that allows everyone to share in defining how these different visions are reconciled.

In addition to consensus making, public spheres play another role that is crucial to social progress: by engaging the maximum number of minds and eyes on any particular problem, solutions are more likely to be found. Dialogic politics are continually engaged in a search for better ways forward, and since no one group holds a monopoly over wisdom (or even knowledge and information), these journeys must be democratic. Democracies are 'long-term experiments in the capacity of citizens to live without secure foundations. We are all required to practice daily the art of living on the edge'.[9] Only politics, as Machiavelli famously taught, creates the possibility for manoeuvre and forward movement. The public sphere is important because it surfaces alternatives – new answers to old questions, challenges to the orthodox, and the occasional revolutionary surprise. In this sense, civil society signifies the 'freedom to imagine something different', for, as Oscar Wilde once quipped, 'a map of the world without Utopia marked on it is not a map worth having'.[10] It is no accident that the World Social Forum picked 'another world is possible' as its organizing slogan.

In the public sphere, all ideas and opinions are valid until proven otherwise. Totalitarianism, by contrast, replaces debate about the merits of an argument with an inquiry about the motives of the individuals involved – the tactic used by Stalin to silence intellectuals in Russia. Margaret Thatcher's infamous double dicta – that 'there is no alternative' and 'no such thing as society' – are natural bedfellows, since in the absence of social networks and associations no 'room' for argument exists. Theories of the public sphere also stress the diffusion of power that is essential to democratic debate and the exercise of accountability by citizens over government, business and their own associations. Accountability requires an active conversation between these institutions and the public (whether as clients, members, citizens or consumers), along with the high levels of transparency and the free flow of information that enable abuses to be exposed. Restrictions on the flow of information will damage the public sphere severely.

Most important of all, the public sphere helps different groups to find a balance between personal autonomy and the demands of the social whole, thus resolving the dilemma that has lain at the heart of civil society thinking since the days of the ancient Greeks. As previous chapters have shown, civil society is the land of difference, the place where we find meaning in our lives as people of different faiths, races, interests, perspectives and agendas. But the governance of complex societies and the preservation of peaceful coexistence require that some of these particularities are surrendered to the common interest, in the form of rules, laws, norms and other agreements that cut across the views of different communities, and to which all citizens subscribe. The application of these rules is ultimately the task of government and other institutions of the state, but civil society also plays a role in both legitimizing government intervention and imposing its own informal settlements through voluntary codes of conduct and other self-organizing principles. Without a functioning public sphere, neither would be possible, since no mechanisms would exist to negotiate the formal and informal rules of the social game.

A successful civil society is one that supports the peaceful expression of these multiple identities without fracturing into a myriad of disconnected agendas – the place where we can celebrate our differences within a common commitment to the interests of a public. As an (admittedly parochial) exemplar, take the case of the Church of the Holy Apostle in Manhattan, which every Friday meticulously clears away all Christian symbols before handing over to the local, but temporarily homeless, Jewish Congregation of Beth Simchattorah for the sabbath. They in turn take equal care to return this space to its owners after their worship has been completed, providing, in microcosm, a vision of a public sphere in which different communities can practise their own rituals while sharing in the common resources provided by the building, carefully maintained by each for the other. These principles operate at higher levels too. Only by reaching out beyond our particularities – by voting for someone from a different group, appreciating the literatures and customs of different traditions, and speaking, literally and metaphorically, many different languages – do we qualify as members of a wider whole. Otherwise, civil society remains the mere agglomeration of different interests. This is why philosophers from Hannah Arendt to Michael Walzer have seen moral maturity as a willingness to welcome diversity *and* seek the common good together among citizens whose interests, at least sometimes, reach further than themselves and their familiars.[11] Dispositions of this kind rest on the formation of democratic identities broad enough to respect differences when they are healthy and attack them when they are not, like racism, sexism, homophobia and a failure to value the lives and life chances of others as dearly as one's own. And public spheres provide the venues for deliberating over which differences fall into each of these camps, going beyond a shallow interpretation of pluralism (defending our differences against each other) to forge a common yet inclusive framework of norms and values. In civil society, difference may be central or irrelevant, something to be celebrated or a cause of deep concern. The goal is to ensure that all decisions about the *meaning* of difference are democratic.[12] This is why inequality and discrimination are enemies of the public sphere, and why fundamentalism, especially when expressed in violence, is the most dangerous enemy of all. Fundamentalists of all persuasions refuse to accept that shared truths can be negotiated or that different versions of the truth can coexist – read blind obedience and absolute righteousness as the mirror image of dialogic politics. Such attitudes violate the basic rules of engagement of the public sphere as a place where 'strangers can meet each other and not draw the knife', a haven for non-violent zones of incivility, and a society that is constantly at war with itself, but peacefully.[13]

At the level of associations, the public sphere is also the place where NGOs and other civic groups confront their own identity as 'special interests' (the charge that is increasingly levelled at them as part of the backlash cited in chapter 1) or 'public interest' groups, defined by Jeffrey Berry as a group 'that seeks a collective good, the advancement of which will not selectively or materially benefit the membership or activists of an organization'.[14] Under this definition, groups working for women's rights in general would qualify, but those working for the rights of one particular group of women might not, unless the claims of that group could be shown to be non-competitive (in other words, that by advancing their interests one would not violate the equal claims of other groups of women). NGO lobbying for better public transport would qualify, but lobbying for a particular rail or road route might not, and so on. This is sensitive and slippery territory for NGOs since the boundary between special and general interests is always porous, and open to very different interpretations. Corporate lobbyists are clearly special interests, but what about business associations that do not privilege one firm over another? Is a stance in favour of global democracy different from one against globalization (the shift that the World Social Forum and its affiliates are currently making), or are both in the public interest? These are questions best left to the public sphere itself.

Threats to the public sphere

In recent years, laments for the decline or erosion of the public sphere have grown more urgent, and the blame is usually laid at the doors of Rupert Murdoch and other media barons.[15] This is unsurprising, since such threats emerge most obviously from the increasing commercialization and concentrated ownership of the media and other vehicles for free expression, and from state control of the media in authoritarian settings when combined with restrictions on basic rights of information and association, especially in the aftermath of 11 September 2001 and the ensuing 'war on terrorism'. Independent investigations of news coverage of the terrorist attacks on New York and Washington DC concluded that journalists on *Time* and *Newsweek* were unwittingly complicit in government communication strategies designed to rally public support, not to facilitate a public debate.[16] But there are many other problems – a tendency to lowest-common-denominator consensus, sound bites and slanging matches as a substitute for rigorous debate, the distortion of politics by money, over-specialized and elitist education systems that turn out 'idiots savants', inequalities in public voice and participation, a narrow interpretation of intellectual property rights that favours business over open access to ideas, and the effects of the modern capitalist economy in reducing the time and energy most people can devote to active citizenship (it being difficult to 'engage in the public sphere' after a twelve-hour or two-job day without any help with childcare). When the pressure is on, most of us succumb to the temptations of 'couch potato' life, in front of the television. All of the things that are required to animate the public sphere are under constant threat – energetic and knowledgeable citizens, independent networks and associations through which they can engage with each other, and the breadth and depth of the forums and arenas in which these engagements take place. The result is that the public sphere cannot function effectively in resolving public-policy dilemmas – like healthcare and social security, for example, in the USA, or an effective system for the peaceful resolution of disputes at the international level. Instead, these dilemmas remain embedded – sometimes frozen – in polities that cannot solve them.

The underlying problem here is a general one – the privatization of the 'public' in every sphere of life and the 'pillaging of that which belongs to all of us' in favour of private interests, whether it be unspoiled open spaces, clean air, genetic diversity, the Internet or the processes of politics themselves.[17] In this context, it is not surprising that the communicative structures of the public sphere have met with a similar fate, but the effects of this process should not be exaggerated. The market share of the fifty largest media corporations in the USA in 1997 was only slightly higher than in 1986, though Rupert Murdoch's control over 35 per cent of newspaper circulation in the UK and Silvio Berlusconi's ownership of three out of four private broadcasting stations in Italy are certainly worrying.[18] What really sets the alarm bells ringing are mergers like those that created AOL Time Warner, Disney and Bertlesmann, since – by bringing different elements of the communications chain together under one authority – they threaten the independence, diversity and diffusion of power that are essential if the public sphere is to operate as theory predicts. The unwillingness of many governments to regulate these mergers and monitor their implications makes this situation even worse, despite the fact that most physical structures of communication – like cable and telephone wires – run along public rights of way. It cannot be accidental that – as in the USA during 2002 – there is little or no coverage of campaign-finance reform measures that would halt political donations from broadcasters and that a portion of the proposed legislation that would cost broadcasters millions of dollars in lost revenues is stripped after intense lobbying from the telecommunications industry. Or that proposed global agreements on 'trade-related intellectual property rights' have been so heavily pushed by telecommunications and media lobby groups like the Motion Picture Association of America and the US-based International Intellectual Property Alliance, along with corporations like AOL Time Warner and Microsoft.[19] The US Congress has already extended the terms of copyright eleven times in the last forty years.

In similar vein, Larry Lessig argues that the increasing commercialization and private ownership of the codes and architecture of the Internet by Microsoft, AOL and others will destroy its potential as a source for innovation. Despite the potential of the Internet and information technology in general as 'great levellers' (reducing the costs of public deliberation and the amount of time and energy citizens must commit), the reality seems to be a degree of Balkanization that mirrors the fractures and particularities we see in other, more traditional, structures of communication. 'You'd be hard pressed to find a group on the Internet committed to the general common good.'[20] The rapid expansion in access to information technology that has enabled NGOs to form influential global campaigning networks over the last five years has not yet been translated into the development of public spheres committed to resolving social and economic problems across societies. And there are other problems that increasingly affect public and private media alike – a general dumbing down of content, for example, the lure of celebrity rather than a commitment to explore the issues that affect

the lives of ordinary citizens, and overly aggressive inter-
viewing techniques that are a million miles away from the
rational discourses envisaged by Jürgen Habermas. 'Don't
try to refute your opponents, just silence them through
intimidation.'

When communications are privatized, the possibilities of
negotiated consensus decline, opening the way for conflicts
between different versions of the truth sustained by their
own exclusive structures of discussion, scholarship and journalism. Something of this sort happened in the Balkans after
the death of Marshall Tito, when press reporters, radio and
television covered the same stories from the perspectives of
the different Yugoslav republics. When war began in Croatia
and soon spread to Bosnia, Croats became *Ushtashe* to
the Serbian media, Serbs became 'Chetniks' to the Croats,
and Muslims became 'Islamic fundamentalists' to reporters
everywhere.[21] As the structures of communication became
fragmented along ethnic lines, mutual stereotypes played an
important role in channelling ancient hatreds into large-scale
violence. What disappeared (and is still absent from the
region despite foreign aid to media projects that stretch
across these divisions) were forums and media directed
at creating precisely those sensibilities that occupied
Rabindranath Tagore in nineteenth-century Bengal – public
spheres broad and inclusive enough to bind different groups
together in some common cause.

In addition, one of the legacies of the civil society revivalists has been a particular understanding of 'civility' as polite-
ness, and the conflation of civil society with 'consensus', not
debate or disagreement. US president George W. Bush, for
example, wants to 'lower the political temperature' in Con-
gressional debates over Iraq by conducting them 'with all
civility', but this is a distortion of what civility originally
meant. Civility, from Aristotle to Stephen Carter, assumes
that we will disagree, often profoundly, but calls on us to
resolve our disagreements peacefully. Everything else – from
street protest to satire – is welcome in the public sphere.
Active citizens need suspicious minds to probe and

challenge, minds that are unafraid of speaking truth to power whenever that is needed. Avoiding debate is never the sign of a robust civic culture (political controversy is educative in and of itself), just as recoiling when challenged is not the quality of good citizens. Nina Eliasoph, a sociologist who has studied the conversations of volunteers in America, found that public debates about politics were frowned on as 'divisive' or 'uncivil', so that people's most important thoughts were relegated to their private interactions.[22] With attitudes like this it is not surprising that democracy is in trouble. The real exemplar of civility is not Miss Manners but Rosa Parks, someone who was brave enough to activate her citizenship in the public interest on a segregated bus in Montgomery, Alabama, even at the risk of being extremely 'impolite'.

America's love–hate relationship with identity politics does not help, leading to all sorts of contortions about what can be said about whom and how, without landing those concerned in court. Political correctness can, of course, be seen as a crucial defence against racism, sexism, homophobia and verbal violence, and a positive affirmation of the value of diversity. But when taken to extremes (when difference cannot be named as the issue, or not the issue, on its own terms), it can have a deadening effect on the quality and depth of public engagement, resulting in a superficial consensus because people from different groups fear to 'read each other's stories', still less understand and internalize their implications for a life lived in common. This is especially true when ideas are sanitized to remove references that may offend on grounds of race, politics or religion – as in the celebrated case of the English exams in New York State exposed by Jeanne Heifitz during 2002.[23] When arguments are curtailed too early, the public sphere can produce an illusion of agreement that disguises differences by class and income, race and gender, excluding the unorthodox and eliding ideological fractures in ways that are convenient for those in authority. People in power, whoever they are, can bear little of the truth as told to them by others or those within society who happen to be different.

These problems are all significant, but perhaps even more important are the pervasive inequalities that threaten the very foundation of the democratic public sphere. At this point in the argument it is important to be honest about the reality of dialogic politics and public interaction, not just the theory. That reality is one of continued, entrenched inequality in voice and access, and the domination of certain orthodoxies over others, which legitimizes ideas through raw power instead of through the power of rational argument between different but equal actors. This problem removes the central plank of Habermas's theory, since it allows one group to impose a particular interpretation of the public interest over others. That fact that all public spheres are fractured by inequality is another reason why a single, unified public sphere or determination of the public interest is difficult to envisage, and perhaps may even be undemocratic in and of itself. Nevertheless, if social realities do obstruct the workings of the public sphere, what actions can be taken to 'level the playing field' so that public engagement at least has a chance to operate democratically?

Despite a tendency to do so in some quarters (motivated by the desire to avoid supposedly 'divisive' conversations about politics), one cannot ignore private interests or identities in order to make a public (that would be akin to baking a cake from the icing down). Such interests (which may be perfectly legitimate in and of themselves) have to be acknowledged and moved through systematically via engagement and debate. Nor can groups that have historically been isolated and marginalized be expected to enter the public sphere on equal terms – African-Americans in the USA, for example, Roma communities across eastern Europe, or grassroots groups from Africa in the global public sphere. Strong bridges of public engagement rest on strong bonds of capacity and confidence within communities, especially those that have been subjugated in the past. 'What matters to us', says the Citizen Organizing Foundation in the UK, 'is not consensus, nor even harmony, but a stake in the ongoing dynamic of controversy, resolution and change.'[24] Consensus, for all the reasons explored so far, does matter, but it has to be a real consensus and not simply an agreement between elites. One cannot long for a vibrant public sphere and avoid the political conflicts that drive people into or out of it. The best consent, let's remember, emerges from dissent, not the rosy glow of polite conversation that fuels liberal fantasies about social transformation.

All this spells *contention*. 'The supposed incivility of contemporary politics stems from the twin emergence of civically and politically engaged issue constituencies that have mobilized enough clout to no longer be ignored, and a continuing counter-mobilization among those who rue their rise from marginalization.'[25] Accepting 'incivility', if this is what it is, seems a paradoxical condition for civil society, but it is especially important because the ability to argue is likely to increase the influence of the materially less powerful even when progress in removing these inequalities is slow ('punching above one's weight', in UK Foreign Office terms). Providing more spaces – physical and virtual – in which public engagement is integrated is also vital. In the USA today, there are few places where low-income white, black and Latino Americans regularly meet – WalMart supermarkets, Medicare and the county jail are three that still remain, but others (including most civic associations) are highly segregated. This is not because people are less willing to engage with each other, but because the opportunities to make connections outside one's group in public have been diminished. Those who do take part in public discussions must also see some short-term benefits from their involvement, requiring reforms in the political system (like curbing the power of lobbyists) so that there is a genuine chance of influencing politics through participation in the public sphere as well as voting.

Conclusion

These threats to the public sphere are serious, and they are mounting. While some of the long-term trends and implications are as yet unclear (and they are certainly contested), there is no doubt that public spheres cannot operate effectively in protecting the common interest if communication, in the broadest sense, continues to be privatized. Social institutions that support reason – by providing the producers of argument and ideas with some autonomy – have to be protected. This is no idle quest, since protecting space for diversity while negotiating common rules and standards is perhaps the most important question facing humankind in the twenty-first century. If this question goes unresolved, further conflict is inevitable.

Although the theory of the public sphere explains much about civil society and its relationship to democracy, it fails to explain how to deal with the structural factors that determine its effectiveness (like inequality in voice), or how deliberation is converted into formal political decisions, or how public engagement can be reinvigorated through different forms of associational life. Like the other models explored in chapters 2 and 3, this one seems incomplete as an explanation of the challenges facing civil society, either as an idea or as a vehicle for social change. And if that is the case, what still remains to be done to unlock the mystery of the civil society puzzle?

5
Synthesis – Unravelling the Civil Society Puzzle

At this point in the argument it is customary to choose one model of civil society over the others and so terminate the debate. Either one takes the well-worn route of the revivalists (associational life as the key to the good society), or one trudges down the 'road less travelled' (civil society as a puzzle rather than a solution), ending up, after a few turns to the left, in the outer reaches of critical theory, or searching for ways to combine state, market and civil society building into a joint attack on social problems. The good news is that there is no need to treat the civil society debate as a zero-sum game in which one model is accepted to the exclusion of the others, and every reason to embrace a holistic approach that integrates elements of all three schools of thought explored in chapters 2, 3 and 4. This is because civil society gains strength both as an idea and as a vehicle for social change when the weaknesses of one set of theories are balanced by the strengths and contributions of the others, a line of argument that enables us to focus on insights that lead to more effective action rather than worrying in the abstract about which theory is correct. In reality, each of these three perspectives has a great deal to offer.

Visions of the good society help to keep our 'eyes on the prize' – the normative goals of poverty reduction, non-discrimination and the revitalization of democracy that, as chapter 3 pointed out, require coordinated action across many different institutions. Being clear about ends and means helps to guard against the tendency to promote certain institutions over others as a goal in and of itself – voluntary associations over states, for example, or markets over both. However, the vision of the good society says little about how such goals are going to be achieved, and associational life does seem to be an important – if incomplete – explanatory factor in most contemporary settings. As explored in chapter 2, structural definitions of civil society are useful in emphasizing the gaps and weaknesses of associational ecosystems that need to be fixed if they are to be effective vehicles for change. Remember that it was dissatisfaction with both state-led and market-driven ideologies that underpinned the rise of interest in civil society in the first place. Chapters 2 and 3 also stressed, however, the differences and particularities of associational life that generate competing views about the ends and means of the good society. Without our third set of theories – civil society as the public sphere – there would be no just and democratic way to reconcile these views and secure a political consensus about the best way forward. Public spheres enable citizens to sort through their differences and achieve at least a functioning sense of the interests they hold in common so that they can be translated into norms, rules and policies that govern one or another aspect of social and economic life. In turn, a healthy associational ecosystem is vital to the public sphere, since it is usually through voluntary organizations and the media that citizens carry on their conversations.

Each set of theories, then, is related to the others, but not, unfortunately, in any universal or easily predictable way. The truth is that these connections are extremely complex, especially when comparisons are made across very different contexts. Although some theorists posit a direct transmission belt between associational life, positive social norms and the achievement of specific social goals, there is little comparative empirical evidence to support their conclusions, and the evidence that does exist suggests one almighty mess – every generalization has at least ten exceptions, and each lesson learned has at least ten qualifying conditions – the 'ifs', 'buts' and 'maybes' that characterize real social change. Are associational life and the public sphere dependent or independent variables in relation to the good society, or are they either or both depending on the circumstances? Are they 'things' that can be factored into models or by-products of the interaction between politics, economics, culture, social structure and state-building as they operate through the long march of history? As the scale of inquiry increases from the local to the global, the number and range of intervening variables is certain to increase, making these equations more complicated still. So how *does* a strong civil society make society strong and civil? This is the most important question in the civil society debate, but it is also the most difficult to answer, and hence the least explored. What new light does the combination of these three models shed on the civil society puzzle?

Associational life, the public sphere and the good society

How does the shape of associational life affect the health of the public sphere and the goals of the good society, in both of the senses outlined in chapter 3 – the development of generalized social norms and the achievement of particular social objectives? These are probably the most complicated relationships of all, so it is necessary to consider them at some significant length.

In the most general of terms, many studies confirm that democratic consolidation is difficult to achieve without a strong associational ecosystem, since independent associations provide the channels or mediating structures through which political participation is mobilized and states are held accountable by their citizens. Mark Warren breaks down these 'democratic effects' into three categories: supporting public spheres of democratic engagement, encouraging the capacities of citizens for democratic participation and deliberation, and effects that underwrite democratic institutions through representation, legitimization and resistance.[1] The influence of popular movements in helping to overturn authoritarian rule in Africa, Asia and Latin America during the 1980s and 1990s testifies to the importance of these effects even where associations have been relatively weak. Whether democracy delivers other goals regularly identified with the good society – such as poverty-reducing growth and social inclusion – is not so clear cut, though in the long run democracy seems to be better at solidifying the contracts and coalitions that progress demands. There is, at least, no evidence that the reverse is true, in other words, that the economic transformations characteristic of development require authoritarian rule, even if certain countries have experienced such regimes during their transitions (compare South Korea, China and Taiwan, for example, with Botswana, Hong Kong and Mauritius). Recent research on 'social capital' (which is not the same as associational life, though closely related), confirms that the strength, spread and connectivity of social networks does have an important influence in economic terms. World Bank research in Indonesia found that membership in local associations had a bigger impact on household welfare than education, especially if their membership was socially heterogeneous and overlapped with membership in other such groups. There is some evidence that these positive effects hold at the national level too, though this evidence is disputed.[2]

However, there are widely varying accounts of the transmission mechanisms involved in these relationships, with three schools of thought being particularly influential, at least in the USA where the literature is most extensive: the 'civic culture' school (like Robert Putnam) sees associational life in general as the driving force behind the consolidation of positive social norms on which the good society is built; the 'comparative associational' school (like Theda Skocpol) sees particular configurations of associational life as the key to securing policy reforms that the good society requires; and the 'school of sceptics' (like Nancy Rosenblum) disputes the links between 'forms and norms' implied in either of these formulations in favour of more complex interactions between different associational ecosystems and their context. Most of the evidence from Third World contexts comes from studies of the development-NGO sector, which as we have seen is a small subset of civil society and therefore not directly comparable, and most treatments of 'global' civil society ignore these questions completely.[3]

The civic culture school

The arguments of this first school of thought were explored in brief in chapter 2. According to their line of reasoning, 'civic engagement' or 'civic culture' – meaning a composite of associational life and voluntary interaction – are independent variables that provide societies with sturdy norms of generalized reciprocity (by creating expectations that favours will be returned), channels of communication through which trust is developed (by being tested and verified by groups and individuals), templates for collaboration (that can be used in wider settings), and a clear sense of the risks of acting opportunistically (that is, outside networks of civic engagement, thereby reinforcing cooperative behaviour, or at least conformity with 'civic values'). Assuming they are distributed broadly enough throughout the population, these positive social norms will produce a 'society that is civil', and – assuming good people make good democrats – they will also create a constituency to support the social, economic and political reforms that are necessary to combat poverty and discrimination. The emphasis here is on 'generalized social capital', since, even if some of it is used for purposes defined as 'bad', enough will be left over to make its overall effects an influence for the 'good'. Scholars like Putnam back up these hypotheses with reams of data that purport to show that 'social capital' in the USA is declining (particularly traditional forms of civic and political participation), and that as a result, America is heading for a crisis of social break-down, political passivity and economic stagnation.[4]

Putnam's thesis is, of course, a great deal more nuanced and sophisticated than this brief summary suggests. Nevertheless, it has generated a large amount of criticism on empirical grounds (by those who question what has happened over time to different types of association), and conceptual grounds (by those who claim that Putnam draws the wrong conclusions from data they accept). Others criticize the conflation of 'civic' with 'liberal democratic' values (which makes associational life a transmission belt for norms that may be dominant, but not necessarily democratic), and the inversion of causes and effects – arguing that trends in social capital are dependent on factors outside of civil society, not the other way around. A common thread in these critiques is a question that connects Putnam and his colleagues to the second school of thought identified above: how can radically different forms of civic participation produce the same effects? If associational life varies as much as was described in chapter 2, then something magical and mysterious must be happening in society at large to produce the generalized effects that Putnam predicts. The natural extension of this line of questioning is to claim that different associations do indeed have different normative and substantive effects, so that the goals of the good society rest not on strengthening civic participation in general but on identifying which particular forms of participation are both lacking and important. In this sense, the key to the civil society puzzle lies through qualitative changes in associational life, not quantitative movements either 'up' or 'down'.

The comparative associational school

One of the most influential writers in this second school of thought is Harvard academic Theda Skocpol, whose detailed historical studies in America have charted the shift from a 'civic world centered around locally-rooted and nationally-active membership associations' to one centred around

professional advocacy groups and social service providers
that may have large numbers of supporters, donors or clients,
but very rarely members in the true sense of the term.[5] The
associations Skocpol mourns include the American Legion,
labour unions (which claimed over 12 per cent of all American adults as members in 1955), parent–teacher associations
(PTAs, which claimed 9 per cent), and a whole roster of organizations named for forest creatures like elks, moose and
eagles (sadly no one seems to have organized around rac-
coons, bats or skunks). Because they represented a substantial cross-income and cross-interest social base (though
predominantly white), these associations were able to form
coalitions that were powerful enough to pressure the federal
government to pass a series of reforms that raised basic standards of health, education and welfare across America – like
the GI Bill of 1944. As in successful developers like Kerala,
West Bengal, Botswana and South Korea later in time, associations like these constituted 'highways' between government and citizens along which information, pressure and
accountability could travel. Skocpol's research shows that
such associations have declined dramatically in the USA
since the Second World War – by 43 per cent for the AFL-
CIO for example, 60 per cent for the National Congress of
PTAs, and 70 per cent for the Masons.[6] The result, summarized in the title of Skocpol's 2003 book, is 'diminished
democracy' – an 'advocacy universe that magnifies polarized
voices and encourages class-biased policy outcomes' (that is,
outcomes biased against the interests of the great majority of
the public), and which is the result of combining 'too-ready
routes to participation by small groups of activists with
intense commitments to (often) extreme causes, coupled
with obstacles to routine participation by ambivalent citizens
with everyday concerns'.[7]

Why is the decline of such associations important? The first
reason has already been mentioned – their success in pushing
through broad-based welfare gains has been endangered by
the collapse of cross-class, local-to-national bridges between
civil society and government, as witness the failure of both

Democratic and Republican administrations during the last thirty years to reform the US health, education and welfare systems. It cannot be coincidental that rising inequality and concentrated power in America have paralleled the decline of nationally federated associations such as labour unions. We also saw in chapter 4 how – like rocks in a stream – engagement across interest groups in the public sphere can moderate extremist positions toward a political consensus on difficult reforms, requiring overlapping memberships in different voluntary associations so that civil society can 'escape any particular cage'.[8] In addition, traditional associations tended to be financed through membership dues (not government contracts, philanthropy or foreign aid), which helped to keep members and leaders in close connection with each other, promoted accountability to a social base, and encouraged leadership development among low-income people instead of among elites claiming to act 'on their behalf'. And, since the skills of democracy are best learned through practice rather than in the classroom or by reading fund-raising leaflets sent by mail, the increasing dominance of lobby groups and service-providing NGOs may threaten the norm-generating effects of associations by reducing citizen involvement to cheque or letter writing and attendance at the occasional rally – the 'junk food' of participation as Sidney Verba calls it.[9]

Similar arguments have been made in other contexts too. Community activists in both North and South, for example, argue that grassroots membership organizations that are internally inclusive and democratic are the key to civic life since they encourage direct involvement by disenfranchised groups in economic and political processes, and take on the structural barriers that limit equal participation and the equal distribution of public benefits – groups like the Community Farm Alliance in Kentucky, for example, the People's Rural Education Movement in Orissa, India, and the landless movement in Brazil. Ashutosh Varshney's work on inter-communal conflict in Indian cities like Ahmedabad suggests that one particular configuration of associational life –

organizations that tie together the interests and activities of Hindus and Muslims – is the crucial factor in preventing outbreaks of inter-ethnic violence, and managing riots successfully when they do break out.[10] When associations are composed exclusively of one ethnic group then they cannot mediate in the interests of the whole (think Rwanda, Lebanon and the Balkans as well as India or northern Nigeria). But when organizations deliberately bring different groups together – like the neighbourhood peace committees Varshney studied in his work – then negotiated settlements are possible.

The common theme of these studies is that the shape of associational life matters greatly in determining the influence of civil society on broader social goals, partly through effects on the health of the public sphere, and partly through effects on positive social norms. These are powerful arguments, but not, I think, conclusive. Varshney's work has been criticized by other scholars who cite changes in employment and industry, migration and state responsibilities in India as just as important to the incidence of conflict as civic life per se.[11] The cross-constituency membership associations lauded by Skocpol and the grassroots groups praised by social activists are not guaranteed to secure the goals of the good society, especially if measured by the achievement of universal rights. As she herself admits, the great protest movements of the 1960s for civil and women's rights did not fit her model, since although new membership associations were vital – like the Southern Christian Leadership Council and the Student Non-Violent Coordinating Committee – such movements were driven forward by a combination of grassroots protest, radical activism, and professional lobbying, not by traditional cross-interest associations like PTAs and the American Legion. And although whites did play a role in the civil rights movement, the movement was overwhelmingly African-American in character, just as the women's movement was driven by women and the gay rights movement was driven by gays and lesbians. The fact that all three movements achieved substantial gains shows that associations that represent a particular constituency can be just as effective in achieving the goals of the good society, if not more so – unless perversely, equal rights are not included. Citing 205 cases of socially progressive legislation passed by the US Congress between 1963 and 1991, Jeffrey Berry concludes that the growth and influence of Washington DC-based 'citizens' lobby groups' is good for democracy and the public interest. 'These are not thin citizens', he says, 'but full-bodied activists, and the nation needs more of them, not less.'[12] People who join such groups are more likely to participate in other aspects of the political process (including voting), and be members of other groups where they do more than write a cheque – helping to produce those overlapping memberships that all schools of thought see as crucial. The problem lies not with the activities of public-interest lobbying, but with the fact that they empower only some parts of the US population, a problem that is taken up below. Equally, many traditional membership associations did not fight for broad-based social reforms but for narrow concerns like gun ownership (the National Rifle Association grew dramatically when it allied itself with partisan politics in the 1970s) and the prevention of abortion (by the National Right to Life Committee, founded in 1973). The evangelical religious movements that have grown so substantially in the USA and elsewhere also tend – unlike Protestant churches in the past – to channel their members' commitments into intra-congregational rather than community-wide activities and concerns.[13]

The school of sceptics

These qualifications have been elaborated in great detail by my third school of thought, which consists of writers who accept that the structure of associational life is shifting in important ways to suit a rapidly changing context, but deny that these shifts have any a priori consequences. In part, this is because new routes to participation are expanding even while older ones are in decline. *Pace* Putnam ('kids today just aren't joiners'), soccer clubs, environmental organizations, self-help groups, churches and the anti-globalization movement are exploding, and many of these newer associations – which Skocpol dismisses as professional lobbyists – do have large numbers of members (the Sierra Club for example, or the National Organization of Women).[14] Some – like the American Association for Retired Persons – also involve them in activities beyond cheque writing, and even in organizational governance. So while the decline of traditional associations may have some negative consequences, the rise of associational life that is more inclusive overall (even if previously excluded groups have to organize around their own interests, at least initially) is surely a good thing. As stressed elsewhere in this book, strong bridges require strong bonds. Changing patterns of civic life may simply reflect a necessary reordering so that civil society remains a positive force as circumstances change. In this school of thought, the key to the civil society puzzle lies in making the connections between the changing structures of associational life in general, the particular effects of individual organizations, and factors in the external context, interactions that defy easy categorization or generalization since all the variables in the equation are mutually dependent.

Following this line of argument, one would not expect any necessary correlation between the characteristics of associations and their normative effects, a reality that is recognized even by the godfathers of compassionate conservatism like John Dilulio, former director of the White House Office of Faith-Based and Community Initiatives. 'We do not know', he says after reviewing ninety-seven rigorous studies of faith-based civic associations and their work, 'whether America's religious armies of compassion . . . necessarily out-perform their secular counterparts.'[15] Research by scholars in the USA like Deborah Minkoff and both Mark Warrens (yes, there are two of them, each working separately on civil society and politics), shows that contentious organizations regularly foster norms of democracy and cooperation, since when people secure their rights and entitlements they become more willing to collaborate with others.[16] Minkoff's work shows that the most effective non-profit organizations are, in any case, 'hybrids' that combine elements of advocacy, service-provision, capacity building and political action – they are rarely 'one thing or the other'. 'Congregations', as David Campbell puts it, 'are not just contractors but sites and resources for church based coalitions and organizing networks' that play an increasing role in politics as well as service.[17]

The most detailed interrogation of the 'forms and norms' debate comes from Nancy Rosenblum, who finds that the effects of associational life on the moral dispositions of their members, and hence on the health of democracy, are complex, fluid and often surprising.[18] Associations that are often dismissed by neo-Toquevillians – like self-help and identity-based groups or street gangs of young people – may have important democratic effects, since, even though their members, resembling Narcissus, may only talk about themselves, at least they take turns in doing so, learning in the process a little of the reciprocity that underpins cooperation and active citizenship. This is an important observation, given that such self-help groups (like Alcoholics Anonymous and Weightwatchers) had over 25 million members in the USA by 1996.[19] Conversely, associations that are singled out for neo-Tocquevillian praise have a mixed and often disappointing record as schools for participatory citizenship, since participation may not extend beyond the group and into the wider world of politics. Associational cultures are diverse and often contradictory, but they may still produce important benefits by articulating neglected voices in the public sphere or developing new loyalties and capacities among their members. Some small groups have the same problems as large bureaucracies (think dysfunctional families) while others show strong commitments to internal democracy, equity and self-criticism. Only 'hate groups', Rosenblum concludes, are unambiguously negative in their effects.

Therefore, the ideal of civic associations as 'mini-democracies' is not essential to the argument that democracy depends on a vigorous associational life. It follows that legislation to enforce internal structures and characteristics in line with public values is unlikely to be effective – accountability to a social base, for example, or democratic elections of their leaders. Encouraging such qualities may be desirable, but attempting to enforce them may, as Hannah Arendt once observed, be the beginning of a slippery slope to 'totalitarianism as the end point of unremitting congruence'.[20] This is an uncomfortable conclusion for civil society enthusiasts, since it implies that associations can practise undemocratic or discriminatory behaviour and still qualify as members – like the Salvation Army's refusal to hire gay employees. Is the preservation of civil society as a protected zone of pluralism a more important objective than enforcing universal standards in a society that is civil? The public sphere must decide the answer to this question, in court if necessary, as it did when the US Supreme Court forced the Minnesota Jaycees to accept women members in 1984.[21]

Outside the USA, the debate on 'forms and norms' is less well researched, and contexts are much more varied. This makes it difficult to draw comparable conclusions, but those studies that exist suggest a similarly complex picture. Different forms of association, or associations with different characteristics, may have similar effects, and the factors that seem to mark out 'high performers' – like flexibility, accountability and learning – are shared by successful public and private sector institutions too. A recent Ford Foundation study of civil society and governance across twenty-two countries found that associational life does contribute to democracy and state accountability, but not as much as was thought, and only when certain conditions are met – alliances and coalitions between associations, for example, inclusive membership, and independence, including as much domestic funding as possible.[22]

'Values-based' NGOs in developing countries do not automatically perform more effectively, since performance depends on the contexts in which they operate and the goals of the work they do – different organizational structures and characteristics are required, for example, to operate effectively in service-provision, policy advocacy, and capacity building among members or beneficiaries. A clear vision or mission, a balance between economic development and political empowerment, strong vertical and horizontal linkages to draw in resources and connect poor people to public and private institutions, and the multiplier effect of strengthening people's own capacities and leadership are common denominators, but they may not be achievable in authoritarian settings or where resources are in short supply. Even if they are, research in Asia and Latin America has shown that 'we cannot say *a priori* that any one type of organization is inherently more or less responsive to, or representative of, the needs of the rural poor'.[23] Where the empowerment of under-represented groups is top priority, building membership-based, internally democratic associations into social movements is likely to be crucial, but in other contexts more traditional forms of organization may be more important. Many of the global social movements that have emerged during the last decade have experimented with new and less structured forms of internal decision-making, management and accountability, but it is not yet clear whether these innovations have fed through into stronger collective norms or substantive results.[24] As in the case of the USA described above, it is not the presence or extent of associational life that makes the difference by itself, but the character of pluralism and the actual activities of different types of association as they are shaped by history and contemporary context.

Is any generalization possible?

Because they take great care to disaggregate different influences from their results, writers in this third school of thought tend to be the best guides to associational life and its effects, but they leave us with a huge amount of diversity and little by way of general conclusions that could be utilized in practice. So let me offer four preliminary generalizations. First, the nature of these links depends how one envisions the goals of the good society, or more precisely the means by which these goals are realized in practice. The 'civic culture school' sees generalized social norms as the driving force of broader social change and associational life in general as the vehicle through which these norms are strengthened. The 'comparative associational school' sees specific policy changes as the key to the good society, supported by mechanisms in the public sphere that enable the necessary political coalitions to be constructed. Certain forms of association will be important to these reforms, while others may be irrelevant, or destructive. Not so, say those in the 'school of sceptics', since one cannot know in advance whether any sort of association is more likely to produce the effects these other authors claim. In this line of reasoning, the best that can be done is to promote as much associational freedom, capacity and social inclusion as possible, and let civil society sort the rest out for itself.

On closer inspection, these three schools of thought are not mutually exclusive, since the goals of the good society are most likely to be achieved when an enabling environment for all associational life is combined with support for specific associational forms that are missing from the civil society ecosystem. So my second generalization is that it is the ecosystem that matters, not the characteristics of its individual components. Overlapping memberships, cross-interest coalitions, hybrid organizations, and the appropriate mix of bonding and bridging, grassroots groups and intermediaries, advocates and service-providers, are more likely to make associational life a handmaiden of broader social progress. Some kinds of association will be crucial to political accountability, but not to trust and cooperation, while others may encourage social norms but have little impact on policy reform. So the stronger, more diverse and independent the civil society ecosystem can be, the greater the chance that these positive interactions will be sustained over time, thus addressing a consistent weakness in the ability of non-state forces to push for continued reforms once the early stages of democratic consolidation have been completed.

Thirdly, within this ecosystem, one kind of organization does seem especially important. These are the associations that, in Martin Luther King's words, practise the 'love that does justice', encouraging their members or supporters to live up to their social obligations as well as their individual moral values, connect their 'individual life worlds to public spaces, encourage collective judgments, and create networks of communication'.[25] The combination of these two levels of action – the individual and the structural – seems best suited to building the dispositions that are crucial both for democracy and for the good society, meaning a willingness to care for the common good and to address the barriers that stand in its way. Here, the moving force is social energy specifically directed at problems of injustice and exclusion, not generalized social norms. Associational life that ignores the structures of power or substitutes for state responsibilities is unlikely to contribute very much to these crucial dispositions.

Fourth, a level playing field for citizen action is critical to the forms–norms link, since otherwise the public sphere cannot operate effectively and associational life, even when effective, will privilege some groups at the expense of others. 'The decisive element in social action is the exercise of power', writes James Luther Adams, 'and the character of social action is determined by the character of the power expressed.'[26] The problem is that these conditions – equality, diversity, independence and a supportive context for citizen action – cannot be obtained by civil society acting alone. Rather, they must be anchored in the broader setting of the good society, where associations are the dependent variable and government or market action are determinant.

The good society, associational life and the public sphere

Freedom, democracy and equality before the law are generally taken to be characteristics of the good society, not just in their procedural or liberal-democratic forms but – across many different cultures and expressions – as basic aspects of human integrity and functioning. The achievement of these conditions has important consequences for non-state action, so the good society is likely to influence the health of the public sphere and the shape of associational life just as much as they, in turn, affect macro social goals. The relationships between civil society in each of its guises are reciprocal. Take equality and independence, two of the conditions already deemed essential to the proper functioning of civil society as a force for positive social change. In chapter 3, we saw how difficult it is for voluntary associations to address the structural problems of inequality, discrimination and the institutionalized concentration of social power, since the guarantor of universal rights and entitlements has to be the state. Only countervailing structures of authority can introduce increasing reciprocity into the general constitution of a society in which serious asymmetries exist. So government action is vital if associational life and the public sphere are to generate both equal opportunities for private interest to be represented and a genuine sense of the public interest too. Otherwise, only certain voices, interests and associations will be heard. This is especially important because there is a close correlation between unequally distributed social resources and the negative functioning of these networks and associations. Relationships between equals, remember, are the raw material of trust, since only from security do people reach out and make connections with others. Social, economic and political equality are therefore preconditions for the ability of civil society to nurture consensus, encourage collective deliberations, and achieve democratic outcomes in which all can participate fairly.

Calls to 'participate more', however, often ignore the economic difficulties that strip people on low or insecure wages of the time and energy to do precisely that, especially when privatization shifts ever greater burdens onto voluntary associations, families and women in the absence of a welfare state. If people feel exploited by the economic systems in which they work, ignored by the political systems in which they vote, and excluded by social systems that discriminate by race, gender or sexual orientation, it is not surprising that 'exit' often seems a better option than 'voice'. The fact that they do still participate, volunteer and organize is obviously a cause for celebration, but it cannot be taken for granted. It is governments' responsibility to deal with the root causes that keep citizens from participating, and participating equally, in associational life and the public sphere, and that means market regulation as well as legislation to promote security and the guaranteed satisfaction of basic human needs. Economic segregation in labour and housing markets separates citizens from one another and makes civil society alliances much more difficult to cement, just as the changing structure of work makes organization and collective bargaining much more difficult. This may be one reason why the current wave of democratization in much of the world is not producing results in welfare and redistribution of the kind that occurred in earlier waves after 1945. Hence 'a more assertive labor movement would do more to revive civil society than any amount of moralizing about the bad habits of the poor'.[27] It is easy to forget that women played a major role in American voluntary associations in the nineteenth century in part because they were disenfranchised in the formal political sphere, or that it took the Civil Rights Act of 1964 to legitimize attempts by voluntary organizations to advocate legally for political equality, not just to break down racial segregation in associational life and cross-race coalitions. Was it accidental that the Reagan administrations of the 1980s demobilized social movements through budget cuts and challenges to non-profit status among advocacy groups, just as the administration of George W. Bush is emphasizing civil society's service-delivery role? These tactics have become routine in many other countries. Whether by design or default, governments can have profound effects on the shape of associational life, for good or for ill, and the outcomes associated with civic engagement in liberal theory are obviously contingent on the political context of a democratic government. 'Good government creates good citizens', as a Palestinian activist put it to researcher Amaney Jamal, not the other way around.[28] In the absence of good government, associations, as in Palestine, may simply be co-opted into patron–client relationships.

Nowhere is this clearer than in the need for legal protection of freedoms of association, speech and information, and for a government-brokered balance between the rights and responsibilities of non-profit organizations in systems of formal accountability. The central importance of independence has been a common theme in the argument to date, since if associations are beholden to business interests or the state, or if the public sphere is captured by commercial concerns or the demands of official secrecy, then their roles may be fatally compromised. This causes obvious difficulties for civil society in authoritarian settings, or in contexts like Islam where state and society (or government and religion) are inextricably intertwined. In these settings, independent oversight of power and authority may be impossible, though accountability mechanisms can still operate at other levels and in other ways. Iranian president Mohammad Khatami, for example, is supportive of a greater role for citizens in discussing the politics of an Islamic state even while the prospects for Western-style voluntary associations remain bleak. For many progressive Muslims, the absence of civil society in the Islamic world is the result of a political conflict between oppressed and oppressor, not a religious conflict between Islam and the West.[29]

Hence, the solutions to any perceived malaise in associational life – as well as many of the problems – lie outside of civil society in actions by governments and by business. This is why consensus on those actions is a vital part of solving the civil society puzzle, an observation that returns us once again to civil society in its role as the public sphere.

The public sphere, associational life and the good society

As we have seen, public spheres are important both because they surface potential solutions to good society problems, and because they mobilize constituencies in support of these ideas. Since a good deal of space has already been taken up with exploring these effects we can simply remind ourselves that a functioning public sphere is therefore vital to associational life and the goals of the good society. Public spheres provide the spaces within which associations articulate their interests and objectives, enabling groups to sort through their differences and legitimize a consensus that is just and democratic. Governments and business, as the saying goes, 'have the right to do what they do, but publics have a right to be offended by it', and use those concerns to pressurize for change. Adam Seligman goes so far as to claim that contemporary societies have the opportunity to resolve the 'two poles of the civil society dilemma (group based ideas of the good versus universalistic claims of human rights) in a way that has not been possible since the mid-Eighteenth Century'.[30] A democratic public sphere is central to this claim.

Conclusion

An integrated approach to civil society that unites elements of all three models increases the utility of this idea both as an explanation and as a vehicle for action. Standing alone, associational life, the public sphere and the good society are each incomplete. Side by side, there is at least a chance that their strengths and weaknesses can be harmonized, and that all three can benefit from a positive and conscious interaction. An inclusive and well-articulated associational ecosystem can be the driving force of the good society, but the achievements of the good society are what make possible the independence and level playing field that underpin a democratic associational life. Without a functioning public sphere neither would be possible, since there would no space for associations to operate in defining the good society's ends and means. This is just as true at the global level, where states remain the duty bearers of international treaties, transnational networks are essential to enforce compliance, and a global public sphere (sadly lacking to be sure) is required to foster debates about international norms. An integrated approach like this should enable the design of interventions that are more likely to be effective, since – rather than isolating particular parts of the puzzle and failing to see where the other pieces fit – all the relevant factors can be addressed collectively, and in some rational order. What does that mean in practice?

6
So What's to be Done?

In most cases, asking civil society scholars to distil policy and practice from their theories is akin to seeking help on plumbing from the local vicar. An embarrassing silence, followed by the sound of pairs of shuffling feet, is the usual accompaniment to the obvious question – so what should we *do*? Those who do attempt to answer this question fall into moral exhortations about improved personal behaviour (a typical response from the 'civil society revivalists'), romantic assumptions about community or movement building (especially common on the left), or – worst of all perhaps – a series of recommendations based purely on what the author thinks the donors and the politicians want to hear. The result is usually an anaemic shopping list made up of NGO capacity building, boot camps for better citizens, and calls to return to some imaginary past where people were nicer to their neighbours and the land flowed with milk, honey and social capital. Robert Putnam's book *Bowling Alone* closes with a long list like this, couched in almost evangelical tones: 'So I set before America's parents, educators . . . and young adults the following challenge . . . that bridging social capital will be substantially greater than it was in their grandparents' era', a task guaranteed to set the pulse racing among teenagers nationwide. It doesn't seem to have occurred to the good professor that 'America's parents' are already confronting such challenges on a daily basis, but in contexts where they get no help from employers or the state, and often little from each other.[1]

In any case, 'what to do' depends on what one understands civil society to be. Devotees of associational life will focus on filling in the gaps and disconnections in the civil society ecosystem, promoting volunteering and voluntary action, securing an 'enabling environment' that privileges NGOs and other civic organizations through tax breaks, and protecting them from undue interference through laws and regulations that guarantee freedom of association. Believers in the good society will focus on building positive interactions between institutions in government, the market and the voluntary sector around common goals such as poverty reduction, human rights and deep democracy, and collective strategies to reach them. Supporters of civil society as the public sphere will focus on promoting access to, and independence for, the structures of communication, extending the paths and meeting grounds that facilitate public deliberation and building the capacities that citizens require to engage with each other across their private boundaries. Those who see civil society as an independent variable will try to build it directly, while those who see it as a by-product of other forces will try to manipulate them in order to produce the best outcomes overall. And if, like me, you see virtue in all these approaches, then the logical thing to do is to look for interventions that seem to strengthen the positive interactions between the different models that were cited in chapter 5 – generating *an inclusive associational ecosystem matched by a strong and democratic state, in which a multiplicity of independent public spheres enable equal participation in setting the rules of the game.* An integrated approach like this avoids the tendency to substitute voluntary action for state building or the demands of democratic politics. This will be my approach throughout chapter 6.

The problem is, this approach is also the most complicated for policy and for practice, defying any attempt to find a

'magic bullet' (like more volunteering), and implying measures that are always specific to their time and place. So the
more rigorous we are about the civil society debate, the more
we return to familiar but intractable problems of gender and
race, state–society relations, and the material bases of change.
And the deeper we delve in this way, the more difficult it
becomes to settle on easy answers on what to do, when, and
where. This produces a level of uncertainty – and requires a
level of flexibility – that sits uneasily with the drive for quick
results measured against certain predefined criteria that
motivate donor agencies in the world of foreign aid. 'Civil
society building' is really a 'black box', implying interactions
between all sorts of variables in an ever changing context,
which make associational life and the public sphere a handmaiden of much broader changes in social, economic and
political structures, and vice versa. Some will be visible, some
invisible, and most will be contingent on context and circumstance. Chapter 5 shed some light on how these interactions work in theory, but in practice they are almost
impossible to manufacture. Underlying these complexities is
the thorny issue of whether intervention of any sort can lead
to predictable outcomes, since the more contingent its development, the more difficult it will be to ensure that civil
society leads to any particular ends. The easiest things to
influence (like the number of NGOs in society) are generally the least important, while the most important – like
'civic' values and a commitment to a common life – are the
least amenable to change. And because civil society has many
different faces, Mr Hyde may be the result even where Dr
Jekyll is the objective.

Where does this frightening image leave us? I think there
are two things that can be done to nurture civil society in all
its guises, without falling into reductionism or false universals. The first is to strengthen the preconditions in which
interactions between associational life, the public sphere and
the good society seem likely to be favourable to goals of
peace, democracy and social justice. This means attacking all
forms of inequality and discrimination, giving people the

means to be active citizens, reforming politics to encourage more participation, guaranteeing the independence of associations and the structures of communication, and building a strong foundation for institutional partnerships, alliances and coalitions. The second is to support innovations in associational life that encourage citizen action to operate in service to the good society through the public sphere, rather than becoming simply an end in itself. Instead of returning associational life to the patterns of a bygone era, this requires its reinvention to suit the radically different circumstances of tomorrow and today – no easy task, especially in contexts and cultures that differ in significant ways each from the other. But if both sets of actions are successful, there is at least a chance that civil societies will be better able to shape themselves organically, peacefully and democratically over time. The outcomes may not conform to a single, prior definition, but they will be more sustained and effective as a result.

Building the preconditions for a true civil society

A consistent theme in the argument thus far has been the inability of associational life to cement the foundations of the good society. Only a deeper commitment to equal citizenship and democratic self-government can bring the two together, through, as described in chapters 4 and 5, the consensus-making functions of the public sphere. Remember that the success of each of our three models of civil society is dependent on its interaction with the others. If these interactions are to operate effectively, there are certain things that have to be done almost regardless of the context, focused on the structural barriers that undermine the conditions in which such synergy can develop. Chief among those conditions are poverty and inequality, exclusion and discrimination, which remove the support systems people need to be active citizens and deprive them of the security required to reach out and make connections with others. It may seem perverse to argue that legal protection of equal rights and the provision of jobs with decent wages, adequate help with childcare, fair taxation, access to quality health and education services and a comprehensive social safety-net are interventions aimed at building civil society, but this is precisely what they are, since in their absence both associational life and the public sphere – and by extension the definition and articulation of the good society – are likely to be dominated by certain groups at the expense of others. Guaranteeing these things to all citizens is one of the best ways to ensure that they have the capacities and opportunities required to shape civil society in accordance with their own wishes, rather than those of donors, governments or corporations.

The persistence of serious inequalities and insecurities endangers civil society as a democratic enterprise and places too much influence in the hands of elites. The sharing of space and resources between Christian and Jewish congregations in Manhattan that I cited in chapter 4 works, in part, because both are made up of reasonably affluent participants. It is not too difficult to live a cosmopolitan life from a position of privilege and safety, since the risks involved are minimal and the effort required is less intense. But expecting people on the breadline to share, participate and cooperate as equals is unreasonable unless efforts are also made to create the conditions in which this is the safe and rational thing for them to do. Arguing about politics, and holding power to account, takes both energy and courage, especially when no 'insurance' – legal, social and financial – exists to support you when power fights back. Gun control would be another civil society building tool, since there is nothing so damaging to trust as the fear of being picked off by a sniper at the supermarket.

No doubt 'reasonable people will disagree' on the best way to provide safety, security and equal protection, and the appropriate mix of state, market and voluntary action this involves, but it is difficult to see how, by themselves, either government, business or non-profit groups could achieve the desired results. Institutional complementarity is essential, not substitution – private for public or non-profit for private. This requires that a careful watch be maintained over the effects of privatization and commercialization on civil society in each of its three disguises, and if necessary an active rolling back. Support to 'co-production' – the joint provision of public goods and essential services by the state, firms and community groups working together – creates synergy in the management of local resources and increases a sense of ownership over the results. Seattle, for example, has a Neighborhood Matching Fund through which public and community resources can be pooled, mirroring experiments throughout urban Latin America which give citizens public and private support for their initiatives as well as a role in the budget process and other aspects of governance.

In addition to these economic interventions, governments have the responsibility to guarantee the independence of associational life and the public sphere, conditions that are necessary to their functioning as vehicles for promoting transparency, accountability, dialogue and debate. This is best done through legal protection of civil and political rights, especially rights of information, association and free speech, and by establishing an enabling environment for citizen action and the independent media composed of a judicious mix of fiscal and regulatory structures that can balance freedom and accountability. In practice, most environments fail this test, being overly intrusive and controlling of associational life, especially in authoritarian contexts where the temptation to co-opt citizens' groups and the means of communication is almost irresistible. Even in mature democracies like the USA these temptations are apparent, especially in the security environment which followed the terrorist attacks of 11 September 2001, where 'Muslim charities' are suspected of channelling funds to terrorist groups and public criticism may be seen as unpatriotic. Donations to such organizations fell by 20 per cent after the White House cracked down on Islamic non-profits organizations and the US Treasury Department issued new guidelines for 'anti-terrorist financing' which ask any US charity providing support to an

NGO abroad to determine the identity of all financial institutions with whom it maintains accounts, and to obtain reference letters substantiating whether these institutions are 'non-cooperative in the international fight against money laundering'.[2] The intention here may be laudable, but the net effect may be to deter support for perfectly proper associations in desperate need of help. In any case, government intrusions of this kind can always be used to target groups for political or ideological (rather than legal or regulatory) reasons, which is anathema to a healthy civil society in which different views and voices have a right to be expressed. We saw in chapter 3 how different schools of thought approach the question of 'uncivil society', meaning the existence of associations whose purposes and practices may offend one group or another. There are many ways to deal with this problem, but legislating for 'congruence' – a state-sponsored definition of acceptable behaviour – runs the risk of freezing out more radical voices. A 'concordat' between government and the voluntary sector is a better way forward, laying out mutual rights and responsibilities, backed up by voluntary codes of conduct but leaving as much room as possible for free association. Such concordats are already being tried out in the UK, Canada and elsewhere. It is especially important that citizens can join and leave non-profit groups as easily as possible, since this makes overlapping memberships – whose importance has been emphasized throughout this book – more likely.

In terms of the public sphere, the free flow of information is essential for equal opportunity, consensus building, and the ability of citizens to hold government and business accountable for their actions. Making access to information about finance, employment, and legal rights widely available helps to offset the isolation of excluded groups, and makes it more likely that public policies can be influenced to their benefit. Therefore, public information disclosure laws and a dense network of public (not necessarily state-owned) media and communication channels are priorities, along with more genuinely 'public' spaces of every sort – physical (like markets

and squares, community centres and public libraries, especially if they have free Internet access), virtual (rolling back
the increasing commercialization and centralized control of
the Internet's architecture and codes by a small number of
corporations), educational (building up public universities at
the expense of private), and in the media (through support
to community radio, public television, subsidized cable channels and a diverse and pluralistic press, including the ver-
nacular). Governments can play their part here by regulating
the communications industry in the public interest – for
example, by preventing companies from buying up local
radio stations en masse, as the Clear Channel Corporation is
attempting to do in the USA, insisting that cable companies
finance community access centres as a condition of their
franchise, and subsidizing the satellite costs of public service
broadcasting.

In addition, public engagement needs paths and meeting
grounds where people can form friendships, challenge each
other and forge new alliances and loyalties across their particularities. In Belarus, the Polish Stefan Batory Foundation
is supporting a series of round-table meetings designed to
facilitate dialogue between government, business and non-
profit groups about future directions in society – an obvious
but unprecedented step in an authoritarian context like this.
Mixed schools, colleges and housing projects; joint media
ventures; collective production and marketing organizations
like cooperatives; and the co-management of natural
resources by different groups – all of these things build
bridges across the lines of class and ethnicity and help to
cement new senses of the 'public'.

More broadly, realizing the positive synergy between our
three models of civil society requires reforms in both representative and participatory democracy in order to revitalize
the public sphere, recognize that associations have a legitimate (non-partisan) role to play in the political system, and
strengthen links between citizens and their government.
These are all ways of cementing the relationships that
connect associational life to the decision-making processes

that determine both the vision and the realization of the good society through the structures of the public sphere. In terms of the formal political system, the fact that only 33 per cent of those aged eighteen to twenty-nine in America voted in the presidential election of 1996 (down from 50 per cent in the early 1970s) is understandable if politics are seen as corrupt, ineffective and unrelated to young people's concerns.[3] But the answer to this dilemma is to make government more responsive and to clean up politics via campaign-finance reform, election monitoring and improved voter registration and voting procedures, not to provide yet more escape routes from political engagement. Part of this process has to be the devolution or decentralization of political authority (backed by the necessary fiscal and financial resources) so that citizens can share in the control of all matters except those where higher-order action is required to ensure a fair distribution of power, interests and resources. Bolivia's 'Law of Popular Participation' is a rare effort to institutionalize subsidiarity in this way, and one which has already been instrumental in efforts in that country to reverse the privatization of municipal water supplies. Expanding citizen voice, participation and representation in state decision making generates consensus, trust and social learning, greater accountability and responsiveness in state institutions, and more protection for minority rights and interests.

In both theory and practice, civil society has been a major beneficiary of the rise of direct or deliberative democracy in the last ten years, and making more space for direct participation in the processes that surround formal politics – the processes of the public sphere – is an important part of any agenda for action. Deliberative opinion polls, alternative voting procedures and modes of representation, facilitated debates on major policy dilemmas, and opening more spaces for citizens to be heard, are all important, though obviously dependent on a supportive political context. Classic forms of participation (like town-hall meetings) may be too costly and time-intensive for today's busy citizens – as Morris Fiorina points out, they were originally 'welcome diversions' from a long and lonely New England winter, after the harvest and before the fields were ready to plough.[4] So new forms of participation, perhaps arranged around the workplace or facilitated by information technology, are especially important. At root, any increase in participation is welcome, since we learn to be citizens not through books or training but through experience and action. In contrast to the murky evidence on 'service learning' reviewed below, it is undeniable that participation in non-profit organizations and social movements early in life makes it more likely that people will continue to participate later on.[5]

Promoting stronger ties between civic and political activity in these ways is a risky business, carrying with it the dangers of co-optation and loss of independence, but we saw in chapter 2 why these ties need to operate successfully if political life is to be truly democratic and effective in securing a consensus on good society reforms. Such ties are also controversial, with claims and counter-claims being made on all sides of the political spectrum about how the two spheres connect. There is empirical evidence for and against the proposition that 'civic education' (which is especially popular in schools, among the politicians if not the pupils), participation in volunteering, and other aspects of associational life lead to greater involvement in politics through voting, campaigning, the willingness to stand for election, and the formation of 'political knowledge' that underpins these dispositions later in life.[6] For the USA as a whole the correlation is clearly weak, since voting is extremely low even though volunteering is high (especially among young people), but this picture disguises substantial evidence that, other things being equal, those who participate in associations are more likely to participate in politics. The fact that 'other things' are not equal takes us back to inequality as the first area for civil society intervention, especially in contexts where voluntary activity, deliberately or not, is seen as a substitute for political action. Such fears are often voiced in the USA, where state-sponsored youth and community service schemes like Americorps and Campus Contract have become

a major plank of both Republican and Democratic party plat-
forms. In the intensely politicized environment of the 'war
on terrorism', these programmes – under the new rubric of
'USA Freedom Corps' – have also been influenced by the
agenda of 'homeland security', leading some critics to label
them as 'snitch-corps', designed to train citizens to spy on
each other rather than holding state authority accountable
for its actions. Some Republicans (though thankfully not
Leslie Lenkowsky, chief executive officer of the Federal
Corporation for National and Community Service), even
want to unite all forms of 'national service' under the same
umbrella, including military service, on the grounds that all
involve 'character and nation building'.[7]

Where does all this leave us in terms of our agenda for civil
society action? Civic education, service learning, community
service and expanded modes of informal political participation can certainly be useful, so long as they are not state-
controlled or used as a substitute for reforms in formal
politics or the other interventions already recommended that
get at the broader factors underlying low rates of participation by low-income and minority groups. These measures can
help to build the preconditions for effective interactions
between associational life, the public sphere and the good
society, but they rely on capacities and connections among
associations that must also be developed. And that, as we
shall see, is just as difficult a task.

Facilitating the development of a healthy associational ecosystem

If associational life and its effects are as complicated as
described in these pages, then any attempt to influence them
through foreign aid or government intervention will be
replete with difficulty and danger. Yet the approach of the
civil-society-building industry that has proliferated since
1989 – with some exceptions – resembles a crude attempt
to manipulate associational life in line with Western, and

specifically North American liberal-democratic templates: pre-selecting organizations that donors think are most important (advocacy NGOs or other vehicles for elites, for example, usually based in capital cities), ignoring domestic expressions of citizen action that do not conform to Western expectations (like informal, village- or clan-based associations in Africa and the Islamic world, more radical social movements, or pre-political formations), spreading mistrust and rivalry as fledgling groups compete for foreign aid, and creating a backlash when associations are identified with foreign interests. The creation of public spheres is usually ignored, apart from occasional support to independent media groups and organizations promoting government accountability. Ignoring Ralf Dahrendorf's warning that 'it takes six months to create new political institutions, six years to create a half-way viable economy, and . . . sixty years to create a civil society', project timescales are collapsed to bite-sized two- or three-year chunks and accountability is reoriented upwards.[8] Nurturing civic institutions (which means connections, attitudes and practices, not just organizations) takes the most careful and sensitive accompaniment over long periods of time. By contrast, the aid industry resembles a bulldozer driven by someone convinced that they are heading in the right direction, but following a map made for another country at another time. Even positive developments like decentralization become formulaic, with, for example, elected multi-purpose bodies like local councils replaced by single-purpose user committees for water, forests, health and education once the donors became attracted to a new but no doubt passing fashion.[9]

In the West, voluntary associations are less vulnerable to the vagaries of aid agencies because their funding base is largely indigenous and usually more diverse, though some of the same effects are visible in attempts by governments to shape the sector in line with their own needs and preferences. In poorer countries where the sector is much weaker, the impact may be to distort the authenticity of pluralism by favouring some groups over others with large financial and technical inputs, retarding the development of embedded relationships between states, citizens and their associations, and contributing still further to state retrenchment and market liberalization in contexts where these goals may be completely inappropriate (large parts of Africa, Asia and Latin America come easily to mind). It is not difficult to start up new NGOs (unless one lives in Myanmar or maybe China), a task that fits comfortably with the donor agencies' tendency to focus on the short term and the easily measurable, or to invest in the physical infrastructure of the non-profit sector. But by themselves, these interventions do little. They are not genuine attempts to facilitate the evolution of organic patterns of associational life, but misguided attempts to shape their destiny according to predetermined norms – what Xiarong Li calls 'civil society determinism'.[10] The results are unlikely to be successful. Like the unhappy off-spring of a dysfunctional marriage, their future as independent, self-sustaining entities will always be under threat. External support can be useful as the oil that lubricates the engine of associational life, but it can never substitute for the hand that drives the car.

A range of independent evaluation studies confirms this gloomy prognosis, but why is the record so poor?[11] Donor agencies are rarely held accountable for the impact of their decisions, nor are they forced to be transparent about the theories of social change they employ. If they were, fewer mistakes would be made. These are not unreasonable demands, one might think, but they are shockingly absent from the world of foreign aid. In addition, external agendas are often contradictory, with support for political associations in pushing for democracy offset by support for economic associations pushing for market liberalization (or at the organizational level, support for NGO service provision trumping support for their political and cultural work). While the donors stated their support for 'pluralism' in Bosnia after the Dayton Accords, what they actually sought out and funded was 'cheap service delivery' according to evaluator Ian Smillie.[12] Official (that is, government) aid is tied to the

political agendas of the administration in power, so it would
be naïve to expect an attitude of pure detachment in areas
as politicized as democracy and civil society. This is not to
say that there have been no successes. George Soros's efforts
in eastern Europe (from providing photocopiers for dissidents to launching independent grant-making bodies like the
Stefan Batory Foundation in Poland) have been notable, as
have some of the efforts of the Ford Foundation and other
US foundations, along with international NGOs like Oxfam
and Novib and some of the more enlightened government
donors in Scandinavia, the Netherlands and the UK. Western
aid to Serbia prior to the overthrow of Slobodan Milošević
was generally well conceived and executed, with funds being
channelled to independent media and monitoring groups and
opposition coalitions like the Alliance for Change.[13] The difference, of course, was that such efforts supported a local
movement that was already well organized and had a very
specific objective. In this scenario, small amounts of money
and technical assistance at the right point in time can make
a major difference.

If the record is so poor, what can be done to improve it?
The first rule of thumb is always to look for forms of associational life that 'live' relatively independently in their
context – not just the 'usual suspects'. They may be
conservative-minded mosque associations or the Boy Scouts
in Lebanon (which Samir Khalaf shows are contributing to
the development of tolerance),[14] burial societies in South
African townships (which played key social, economic and
political roles under apartheid), self-help groups in America
(which now outnumber traditional membership associations), or labour unions in France and Brazil (which have
been prime movers in the burgeoning global justice movement). It is groups like these that occupy the frontiers in
organizing new responses to problems of community and
association against the background of globalizing capitalism,
resurgent nationalism, and the fragmentation they breed.
And if, as scholars have demonstrated convincingly, associational life was radically reshaped in the West at the end of

the nineteenth century by urbanization, industrialization and immigration, then it can be reshaped again. The global justice movement has been particularly innovative in developing new and less hierarchical structures, practices and organizing techniques across borders, though it remains to be seen whether these innovations will generate any consensus at the level of specific policy alternatives.

Second, focus on the associational ecosystem by fostering the conditions in which all of its components can function more effectively, alone and together. If the 'soil' and the 'climate' are right, associational life will grow and evolve in ways that suit the local environment. This requires support to as broad a range of groups as possible, helping them to work synergistically to defend and advance their visions of civic life, providing additional resources for them to find their own ways of marrying flexible, humane service with independent critique, and leaving them to sort out their relationships both with each other and with the publics who must support them, and to whom they must be accountable, if their work is to be sustained. Support to civic–political linkages in associational life is also important, including the advocacy role of non-profit groups and their ability to marry different functions together as recommended in chapter 5 – the creation of hybrid organizations that combine service delivery, capacity building and advocacy, or the combined personal and structural changes captured in 'the love that does justice'. 'Service politics' might be considered an oxymoron by some, but it is worth consideration in its ability to pull these two dimensions of citizen action together.[15] Regulatory regimes and the contractual arrangements used by governments when they fund non-profit organizations need to be sensitive to this balance. It is the depth and continuity of this ecosystem that enables citizens to resist authoritarian takeovers and respond to new political opportunities when they arise. Other important measures include support to less visible associations and those representing the interests of marginalized groups (especially women's associations, which have been proven to be better intermediaries

between people and institutions in many Third World contexts);[16] renewing the pipeline of leadership in order to
address the tendency of associations to develop greater
inertia and self-interest over time; and strengthening the connections that link people vertically and horizontally into new
relationships and networks for collective action across in-
group boundaries, whether in broad-based coalitions and
alliances, social movements, or more basic relationships
between intermediary organizations and membership groups
with a social constituency. All these measures will increase
the influence of less powerful groups on public policy as well
as building new and overlapping norms and accountabilities.

Third, focus as much attention as possible on strengthening the financial independence of voluntary associations,
since dependence on government or foreign funding is the
Achilles heel of authentic civic action. Resources always have
a 'steering effect' that must be factored into questions of
organizational identity, function, mission and accountability.
Associations that have a diverse revenue base rooted in local
voluntary contributions are usually better able to resist pressure from governments, keep their sights firmly on their core
activities, and dispel the accusation that they are simply
pawns of outside interests. This does not mean replicating
traditional models of charity fund-raising developed in the
West (the 'starving baby' syndrome), but encouraging a
much broader set of mechanisms including member dues,
cost-recovery for services provided, commercial income,
foundation grants, and endowments. Despite some recent
minor scandals (like the senior executive at the Markle Foundation in New York who visited Fifi La Roo's spa in the
Hamptons on 'official business'), foundation funding remains
especially important because of its flexibility and long
timescales.[17] National and sub-national development funds
(in which different donors pool their resources) also offer
promise.[18]

Finally, because so little is known or understood about civil
society in non-Western contexts, further research on the
realities and complexities of associational life in Islamic and

Confucian societies, sub-Saharan Africa, south Asia and Latin America is very important. More research will not lead to more effective assistance by itself, but at least it will create a better base of information on which donors base their judgements and make it easier to expose – and challenge – the assumptions they often make. In short:

- be clear and transparent about why you are promoting certain patterns of associational life, and take responsibility for the results
- focus on the conditions in which associations can shape themselves and their relationships, not a predetermined view of which forms you think are most important
- think of associational life as an ecosystem and look for components that are weak, absent or disconnected
- provide resources for as broad a range as possible of groups to come together and articulate their own visions of the future
- promote indigenous roots and accountability as the key to effective resource generation, independence and effectiveness.

Conclusion

How large does an idea have to be before it qualifies as a 'big idea'? Does civil society count, or is it too complex and restricted in its relevance to certain contexts and cultures? Civil society, in the ways I have explored it in this book, is certainly an important idea, because it helps us, in good Marxist fashion, to interpret and change the world simultaneously. And given the intellectual alternatives – like neoliberal economics and state retrenchment, nationalism, communism and fascism – it is also an idea that deserves very serious attention. But since there is no consensus about what civil society is, what it does, or even whether it exists in certain parts of the world, it would be foolish to make too many claims, too soon. What seems certain is that civil society will provide a central organizing framework for debate in the next ten years, and possibly beyond.

As I hope to have shown, civil society is simultaneously a goal to aim for, a means to achieve it, and a framework for engaging with each other about ends and means. When these three 'faces' turn towards each other and integrate their different perspectives into a mutually supportive framework, the idea of civil society can explain a great deal about the course of politics and democracy, the achievement of peace and social justice, and the development of norms and values that underpin these things. Theories of the good society help to keep our gaze on the normative goals and institutional challenges that motivate the search for freedom and human progress; theories of associational life help to explain how to meet those challenges through the medium of non-state action, which is always necessary but never sufficient; and theories of the public sphere connect the two together by providing a framework for argument and negotiation around social goals and the strategies required to reach them. Many of the difficulties of the civil society debate disappear when we simply lower our expectations of what each of these schools of thought has to offer in isolation from the others, identify and build on the connections that exist between them, and abandon all attempts to enforce a single model, consensus or explanation.

Building a true civil society in all three ways will take enormous energy and imagination, and this is why the inspiration that this idea provides to popular struggles is so important. At the Djibouti Peace Conference for Somalia in 2000, the language of civil society was used extensively by local forces as a counterpoint to continued rule by warlords.[19] 'What right do you have to take away a concept that we find so important in our work', was the comment made to me by an activist in India in 2002, and quite right too. Whatever its shortcomings in theory, civil society does offer both a touchstone for social movements and a practical framework for organizing resistance and alternative solutions to social, economic and political problems. And because the essence of civil society is collective action – in associations, through the public sphere and across society – this debate reminds us that individual efforts and experiences can never substitute for the relationships of love, solidarity, sacrifice and friendship that are the essence of our true human nature. At a time when such relationships are severely strained by broader changes in society, international relations and the economy, this may be the most important lesson that civil society has to teach.

It is a truism that civil society is what we, as active citizens, make it, but it is also true that 'social energy', or 'willed action', is the spark that ignites civil society as a force for positive social change. The determination to do something because it is the right thing to do, not because we are told to do it by governments or enticed to do it by the market, is what makes associational life a force for good, provides fuel for change in the practices of states and business, and motivates people to raise their voices in the public sphere. While criticisms of civil society are often valid, think what life would be like without the dreams of the good society, the resources and opportunities of voluntary associations, and the arguments and democratic life of the public sphere. No doubt all bowling leagues would be owned by Rupert Murdoch and federal regulations would be issued to every choir master and choir mistress in the land! Against the background of weak democracies, strong bureaucracies, corporate power, legalism and nationalism resurgent, civil society, as both concept and reality, is essential to the prospects for a peaceful and prosperous world order in the twenty-first century, because it 'leads us to a renewed awareness of the fusion of the moral, the social and the political in the constitution of all human communities'.[20]

The hundreds and thousands of people who gathered together at the World Social Forum in Brazil in 2002, and the many millions more who took to the streets to demonstrate against a war on Iraq, provide a useful reminder that mass protest on the basis of human community may yet generate the foundation for alternative forms of politics and a new kind of society. In this conviction at least, I am happy to be called a 'civil society revivalist'. At its best, civil society is the story of ordinary people living extraordinary lives through their relationships with each other, driven forward by a vision of the world that is ruled by love and compassion, non-violence and solidarity. At its worst, it is little more than a slogan, and a confusing one at that, but there is no need to focus on the worst of things and leave the best behind. Warts and all, the idea of civil society remains compelling, not because it provides the tidiest of explanations but because it speaks to the best in us, and calls on the best in us to respond in kind.

Notes

CHAPTER 1 INTRODUCTION – WHAT'S THE BIG IDEA?

1 From an undated fundraising letter signed by Cato Institute president Edward H. Crane and received by the author in 2001. The incentive for contributors was a complimentary copy of *Little Civics Lessons* by P. J. O'Rourke.

2 The quotes in this section come in the order they are written from Eberly (1998: 4–5); the Advocacy Institute's 2001 annual report; Scholte (2002: 2); Boggs (2000: 259); Stephen White, cited in Post and Rosenblum (2002); Seligman (1992); and Rifkin (1995: 280).

3 Hann and Dunn (1996: 1); Chambers and Kymlicka (2002: 1); Khilnani (2002: 11); and Seligman (1992: 169).

4 The late Gordon White (1994: 376).

5 See, for example, Seligman (1992); Keane (1998); Ehrenberg (1999); and Foley and Hodgkinson (2002).

6 Ehrenberg (1999: xi).

7 For a good review of these debates see Cohen and Arato (1992).

8 See the contributions to Post and Rosenblum (2002) and Chambers and Kymlicka (2002).

9 The best summary of these critiques is Edwards, Foley and Dani (2001).

10 Foley and Hodgkinson (2002).

11 Chambers (2002: 94).

12 Chambers and Kymlicka (2002: 8); Cohen (1999); Keane (1998).

13 Bellah (1995: 277).
14 See Edwards (1999a), chapter 3.
15 Salamon and Anheier (1999: 8).
16 See, for example, Harbeson, Rothschild and Chazan (1994); Keane (1988); Escobar and Alvarez (1992); and Fox and Hernandez (1992).
17 Edwards (2000b: 10).
18 Wolfe (1998: 18).
19 The conversation was reported to me by Professor James Manor of the Institute for Development Studies at the University of Sussex.
20 Chandoke (2003); Rieff (1999).
21 From Edwards (2000b: 16).
22 A good summary of criticisms from the mainstream appears in 'Sins of the secular missionaries', *The Economist*, 29 January 2000, pp. 25–7. See also 'The backlash against NGOs' by Michael Bond in *Prospect*, 30 March 2000.
23 Available at <http://www.edelman.com>, 2002.

CHAPTER 2   CIVIL SOCIETY AS ASSOCIATIONAL LIFE

1 Goody (2002: 157).
2 From Engel's foreword to Luther Adams (1986: viii).
3 O'Connell (1999: 125).
4 De Tocqueville (1945: vol. 2, 114).
5 Cited by Luther Adams (1986: 160).
6 Cited by Reilly (1995: 7).
7 Walzer (1998: 124).
8 Post and Rosenblum (2002); Uphoff (1993).
9 Keane (1998: 6, my emphasis).
10 Salamon (1993); Mathews (1997).
11 The statistics in this section come, in the order they are cited, from Edwards and Hulme (1995: 187); Salamon and Anheier (1997, 1999); Robinson and White (1997: 10); Xiaoguang (2002: 5); Edwards and Hulme (ibid.); and Mertes (2002: 4).
12 Putnam (2000: 49, 83, 173, 133); Ladd (1999: 29); Skocpol (1999); Ray (2002).
13 Knight and Stokes (1996).
14 47,098 to be exact: see Glasius, Kaldor and Anheier (2003: 195) and Edwards and Zadek (2003).
15 Skocpol (1999).

16 Cohen and Arato (1992: x).
17 *The Economist,* 13 January 2001: 42.
18 Antlov (2003).
19 See Foley and Edwards (1996).
20 Hashemi (1997).
21 Edwards and Gaventa (2001).
22 Walzer (1998); Lasch (1996); Cohen and Arato (1992: viii).
23 Edwards (1999a: 94); Varshney (2002); Peters and Scarpacci (1998).
24 Zadek (2001).
25 See Butler (2000).
26 Dawson (2001); F. Harris (1999).
27 Gellner (1994: 103).
28 See Mardin (1995); Ibrahim (1995); Kelsay (2002); Azra (2002) and Zubaida (2002). The example from Turkey comes from White (1996).
29 Bayart (1986); Bratton (1994); Harbeson, Rothschild and Chazan (1994); Mamdani (1996); Comaroff and Comaroff (1999).
30 Howell and Pearce (2001); Nosco (2002); Metzger (2002).
31 De Oliveira and Tandon (1994: 73).
32 Woolcock (1998); Edwards (2000a).
33 Warren (2001); Bebbington (1996). SPARC is described in Patel, Bolnick and Mitlin (2001).
34 *Chicago Sun Times,* 5 November 2002; GPN activists mailing list, 15 November 2002.
35 See Tarrow (1998); and Giugni (1999).
36 Lichtenstein (2002).
37 Skocpol (1999, 2003).

CHAPTER 3   CIVIL SOCIETY AS THE GOOD SOCIETY

1 'Thoughts of the First Accused: Saad Eddin Ibrahim to the Supreme State Security Court, 29 July 2002, case number 13244'. Ibrahim was imprisoned for two periods in 2001 and 2002, released at the end of 2002 and acquitted on 18 March 2003.
2 Roepke (1996).
3 Seligman (2002: 28); Hall (1995); Keane (1988); Gellner (1994).

4   Cited in Myers (1996); Perez-Diaz (1993).
5   *Chronicle of Philanthropy*, 31 October 2002.
6   Cited by Seligman (1992: 2). The definition comes from Walzer (1998: 132), though the emphasis is mine.
7   A term used by McClain and Fleming (2000) to refer to the work of Putnam, Etzioni and others.
8   Rosenblum (1998: 350).
9   Putnam (2000). This anecdote comes from Constance Buchanan, a colleague of mine at the Ford Foundation in New York, who used to work at the Harvard Divinity School. The emphasis is mine.
10   Keane (1998: 45).
11   Galston and Levine (1998: 36).
12   See Robin (2001).
13   Uvin (1998); Salem (1998); Majed (1998); Khalaf (2002).
14   The most recent investigations of the Columbine shootings cast doubt on this finding.
15   The origins of this remark lie in Fareed Zakaria's review of Francis Fukuyama's book *Trust* in the *New York Times*, cited in Levi (1996).
16   Chambers (2002).
17   Geremek (1992); Diamond (1998); Berlet and Lyons (2000).
18   Keane (1998: 50).
19   Seligman (1992: 197–8).
20   Verba, Schlozman and Brady (1995: 457).
21   Cohen (1999: 79).
22   Carter (1999: 230).
23   Cited in Reilly (1995: 8). The second quote comes from Rick Cohen, executive director of the National Committee on Responsive Philanthropy in Washington DC.
24   Post and Rosenblum (2002: 3, 8).
25   Cited by Keane (1998). The second quote comes from Rieff (1999: 12).
26   On Kerala see Heller (1996) and J. Harris (2001). On state–society synergy more broadly see Evans (1996), Tendler (1996) and Edwards (1999a, chapter 3).

CHAPTER 4   CIVIL SOCIETY AS THE PUBLIC SPHERE

1   Cited in Chatterjee (2002).
2   Rosen (2001).

3 McClain and Fleming (2000).
4 Keane (1998).
5 Ibid.: 169.
6 <http://www.opendemocracy.net>.
7 Cited in McConnell (2003: 41). See also Hampshire (1999).
8 Etzioni (1993: xi).
9 Keane (2001).
10 Howell and Pearce (2001: 237).
11 Arendt, cited in Myers (1996: 4) and Walzer (1998: 303).
12 Jordan (1992: 197).
13 Keane (1998).
14 Berry (1999b: 190).
15 See, for example, Boggs (2000), Bollier (2001) and Lessig (2001).
16 University of Washington Newsletter (Seattle), September 2002.
17 Bollier (2001).
18 Compaine 2002; Communication Rights in the Information Society (2002a).
19 Center for Public Integrity (2002); Communication Rights in the Information Society (2002b).
20 Lessig (2001); Levine (2002).
21 See J. Peklo, *The Balkan Syndrome: Nationalism and the Media*, ZNAK Foundation, Krakow, Poland.
22 Eliasoph (1998).
23 'The elderly man and the sea?', *New York Times*, 2 June 2002.
24 Cited in Douglas and Borgos (1996).
25 Edwards and Foley (2001: 139).

CHAPTER 5   SYNTHESIS – UNRAVELLING THE CIVIL
SOCIETY PUZZLE

1 Warren (2001), *Democracy and Association*.
2 Grootaert (1999); Pritchett and Kaufman (1998).
3 Contrast Keane (2003) and Kaldor (2003), for example, with Edwards (2000b) and the contributions to Edwards and Gaventa (2001).
4 Putnam (2000).
5 Skocpol (1999).
6 Ibid.: 475.

7   Skocpol (2003); Fiorina (1999: 20).
8   Hall (1995: 15).
9   Verba, Schlozman and Brady (1995).
10 Varshney (2002).
11 Van der Veer (2002).
12 Berry (1999b: 389).
13 Wuthnow (1999).
14 Putnam (2000: 15); Ladd (1999); Ray (2002).
15 Johnson (2002).
16 Warren (2001) *Democracy and Association*; Warren (2001) *Dry Bones Rattling*; Minkoff (2002a and b); and Campbell (2002).
17 Campbell (2002).
18 Rosenblum (1998, 1999); Post and Rosenblum (2002).
19 Wasserman (1999: 240).
20 Cited in Post and Rosenblum (2002: 16).
21 See Galston (2002).
22 These studies can be accessed at the Institute for Development Studies website: <www.ids.ac.uk/IDS/civsoc/map.html>.
23 Bebbington and Thiele (1993: 21); see also Edwards and Hulme (1995) and Edwards (1999b).
24 Mertes (2002). Naomi Klein (2000, 2002) makes much of these claims in her writings.
25 Warren (2001), *Democracy and Association*.
26 Luther Adams (1986: 62).
27 Ehrenberg (1999: 249).
28 Jamal (2003).
29 Kelsay (2002).
30 Seligman (2002: 30).

CHAPTER 6   SO WHAT'S TO BE DONE?

1   Putnam (2000: 404).
2   'US Department of the Treasury anti-terrorist financing guidelines: voluntary best practices for US-based charities (2002)', *Chronicle of Philanthropy*, 6 January 2003.
3   Galston (2001).
4   Fiorina (1999).
5   See Giugni (1999) and Edwards and Foley (2001).

6   For an up-to-date and careful review of this evidence see Galston (2001).
7   Paul Glastris, cited in *Leadership and Service in Times of National Crisis,* Grantmaker Forum on Community and National Service, Berkeley, Ca. (2002).
8   Cited in Khalaf (2002).
9   See James Manor (2002) *User Committees: A Potentially Damaging Second Wave of Decentralization,* Institute of Development Studies, University of Sussex.
10 Li (1999).
11 See, for example, Sampson (1996); Van Rooy (1998); Carothers and Ottaway (2000); Howell and Pearce (2001); and Jenkins (2002).
12 Smillie (1996: iv); see also Hulme and Edwards (1997).
13 Carothers (2001).
14 Khalaf (2002).
15 The term 'service politics' comes from *The New Student Politics: The Wingspread Statement on Student Civic Engagement.* Washington DC: Campus Contract (2001).
16 See the papers by Bebbington and Carroll, Salmen and Reid, and Uphoff and Krishna, all in the World Bank Social Capital Library of works in progress at <http://www.worldbank.org/poverty/scapital/index.htm>.
17 'A Foundation Travels Far from Sesame Street': *New York Times,* 6 September 2002.
18 The model of consolidated development funds is explored in Edwards (1999a) Chapter 7.
19 Lewis (2002).
20 Hann and Dunn (1996: 3).

References and Bibliography

Antlov, H. (2003) 'Not enough politics! Participation and the new democratic polity in Indonesia', in E. Aspinall and G. Fealy (eds.), *Indonesia: Decentralization and Democratization*. Singapore: Institute of South-East Asian Studies.

Azra, A. (2002) 'The challenge of democracy in the Muslim world: traditional politics and democratic political culture', keynote address to the Conference on the Challenges of Democracy in the Muslim World, Jakarta, March 19–20.

Bayart, J.-F. (1986) 'Civil society in Africa', in P. Chabal (ed.), *Political Domination in Africa*. Cambridge: Cambridge University Press.

Bebbington, A. (1996) 'Organizations and intensifications: campesino federations, rural livelihoods and agricultural technology in the Andes and Amazonia', *World Development*, 24 (7), 1161–77.

Bebbington, A., and G. Thiele, eds. (1993) *NGOs and the State in Latin America*. London: Routledge.

Bellah, R. (1995) *Habits of the Heart: Individualism and Commitment in American Life*. Berkeley: University of California Press.

Berlet, C., and M. Lyons (2000) *Right-Wing Populism in America*. New York: Guilford Press.

Berry, J. (1999a) *The New Liberalism: The Rising Power of Citizen Groups*. Washington DC: Brookings Institution Press.

Berry, J. (1999b) 'The rise of citizen groups', in T. Skocpol and M. Fiorina (eds.), *Civic Engagement in American Democracy*. Washington DC: Brookings Institution Press.

Boggs, C. (2000) *The End of Politics: Corporate Power and the Decline of the Public Sphere*. New York: Guilford Press.

Bollier, D. (2001) *Public Assets, Private Profits: Reclaiming the American Commons in an Age of Market Enclosure*. Washington DC: New America Foundation.

Bratton, M. (1994) 'Civil society and political transition in Africa', in J. Harbeson, D. Rothschild and N. Chazan (eds.), *Civil Society and the State in Africa*.

Butler, J. (2000) For faith and family: Christian right advocacy at the United Nations, *Public Eye*, 9 (2/3).

Campbell, D. (2002) 'Beyond charitable choice: the diverse service delivery approaches of faith-related organizations', *Non-Profit and Voluntary Sector Quarterly*, 31 (2), 207–30.

Carothers, T. (2001) *Ousting Foreign Strongmen: Lessons from Serbia*. Washington DC: Carnegie Endowment for International Peace, Policy Brief 1 (5).

Carothers, T., and M. Ottaway (2000) *Funding Virtue: Civil Society Aid and Democracy Promotion*. Washington DC: Carnegie Endowment for International Peace.

Carter, S. (1999) *Civility*. New York: Harper Perennial Books.

Center for Public Integrity (2002) *The Politics and Influence of the Telecommunications Industry*. Washington DC: CPI.

Chambers, S. (2002) 'A critical theory of civil society', in S. Chambers and W. Kymlicka (eds.), *Alternative Conceptions of Civil Society*. Princeton: Princeton University Press.

Chambers, S., and W. Kymlicka, eds. (2002) *Alternative Conceptions of Civil Society*. Princeton: Princeton University Press.

Chandoke, N. (2003) *The Conceits of Civil Society*. New Delhi: Oxford University Press.

Chatterjee, P. (2002) 'Civil and political society in postcolonial democracies', in S. Khilnani and S. Kaviraj (eds.), *Civil Society: History and Possibilities*.

Cohen, J. (1999) 'American civil society talk', in R. Fullwinder (ed.), *Civil Society, Democracy and Civic Renewal*.

Cohen, J., and A. Arato (1992) *Civil Society and Political Theory*. Cambridge, Ma: MIT Press.

Comaroff, John, and Jean Comaroff , eds. (1999) *Civil Society and the Political Imagination in Africa*. Chicago: University of Chicago Press.

Communication Rights in the Information Society (2002a) *Media Ownership: Big Deal?* London: CRIS Campaign, Issue Paper 4.

Communication Rights in the Information Society (2002b) *Why Should Intellectual Property Rights Matter to Civil Society?* London: CRIS Campaign, Issue Paper 2.

Compaine, B. (2002) 'Global media', *Foreign Policy* (November/ December).

Dawson, M. (2001) *Black Visions: The Roots of Contemporary African-American Mass Political Ideologies.* Chicago: University of Chicago Press.

De Oliveira, M., and R. Tandon, eds. (1994) *Citizens Strengthening Global Civil Society.* Washington DC: CIVICUS.

De Tocqueville, A. (1945) *Democracy in America,* two volumes. New York: Knopf.

Diamond, S. (1998) *Not by Politics Alone: The Enduring Influence of the Christian Right.* New York: Guilford Press.

Dionne, E. J., ed. (1998) *Community Works: The Revival of Civil Society in America.* Washington DC: Brookings Institution Press.

Douglas, S., and S. Borgos (1996) 'Community organizing and civic renewal: a view from the south', *Social Policy* (Winter), 18–28.

Eberly, D. (1998) *America's Promise: Civil Society and the Renewal of American Culture.* Lanham: Rowman and Littlefield.

Edwards, B., and M. Foley (2001) 'Civil society and social capital: a primer', in B. Edwards, M. Foley and M. Dani (eds.), *Beyond Tocqueville.*

Edwards, B., M. Foley, and M. Dani, eds. (2001) *Beyond Tocqueville: Civil Society and the Social Capital Debate in Comparative Perspective.* Hanover: University Press of New England.

Edwards, M. (1999a) *Future Positive: International Cooperation in the 21st Century.* London: Earthscan.

Edwards, M. (1999b) 'NGO performance: what breeds success? New evidence from South Asia', *World Development,* 27 (2), 361–74.

Edwards, M. (2000a) 'Enthusiasts, tacticians and skeptics: civil society and social capital', *Kettering Review,* 18 (1), 39–51.

Edwards, M. (2000b) *NGO Rights and Responsibilities: a New Deal for Global Governance.* London: Foreign Policy Centre.

Edwards, M., and D. Hulme, eds. (1995) *Beyond the Magic Bullet: NGO Performance and Accountability in the Post Cold War World.* West Hartford: Kumarian Press; London: Earthscan.

Edwards, M., and J. Gaventa, eds. (2001) *Global Citizen Action.* Boulder: Lynne Rienner; London: Earthscan.

Edwards, M., and S. Zadek (2003) 'Governing the provision of global public goods: the role and legitimacy of non-state actors', in I. Kaul, P. Conceiçâo, K. Le Goulven and R. Mendoza (eds.), *Governing Globalization*. Oxford: Oxford University Press.

Ehrenberg, J. (1999) *Civil Society: The Critical History of an Idea*. New York: New York University Press.

Eliasoph, N. (1998) *Avoiding Politics: How Americans Produce Apathy in Everyday Life*. Cambridge: Cambridge University Press.

Escobar, A., and S. Alvarez, eds. (1992) *The Making of Social Movements in Latin America: Identity, Strategy and Democracy*. Boulder: Westview Press.

Etzioni, A. (1993) *The Spirit of Community*. London: Fontana.

Evans, P. (1996) 'Development strategies across the public-private divide: introduction', *World Development*, 24 (6), 1033–7.

Falk, R. (1995) *On Humane Governance: Toward a New Global Politics*. Cambridge: Polity.

Fiorina, M. (1999) 'Extreme voices: the dark side of civic engagement', in T. Skocpol and M. Fiorina (eds.), *Civic Engagement in American Democracy*.

Foley, M., and B. Edwards (1996) 'The paradox of civil society', *Journal of Democracy*, 7 (3), 38–52.

Foley, M., and V. Hodgkinson (2002) 'Introduction', in M. Foley and V. Hodgkinson (eds.), *The Civil Society Reader*. Hanover: University Press of New England.

Fox, J., and L. Hernandez (1992) 'Mexico's difficult democracy: grassroots movements, NGOs and local government, *Alternatives*, 17, 165–208.

Fullwinder, R., ed. (1999) *Civil Society, Democracy and Civic Renewal*. Lanham: Rowman and Littlefield.

Galston, W. (2001) 'Political knowledge, political engagement and civic education', *Annual Review of Political Science*, 4, 217–34.

Galston, W. (2002) 'Liberal egalitarianism: a family of theories, not a single view', in R. Post and N. Rosenblum (eds.), *Civil Society and Government*.

Galston, W., and P. Levine (1998) 'America's civic condition: A glance at the evidence', in E. J. Dionne (ed.), *Community Works*.

Gellner, E. (1994) *Conditions of Liberty: Civil Society and its Rivals*. London: Hamish Hamilton.

Geremek, B. (1992) *The Idea of Civil Society*. North Carolina: National Humanities Center.

Giddens, A., ed. (2001) *The Global Third Way Debate*. Cambridge: Polity.

Giugni, M. (1999) 'How social movements matter', in M. Giugni, D. McAdam and C. Tilly (eds.), *How Social Movements Matter*. Minneapolis: University of Minnesota Press.

Glasius, M., M. Kaldor, and H. Anheier, eds. (2003) *Global Civil Society 2002*. Oxford: Oxford University Press.

Goody, J. (2002) 'Civil society in an extra-European perspective', in S. Khilnani and S. Kaviraj (eds.), *Civil Society: History and Possibilities*.

Grootaert, C. (1999) *Does Social Capital Help the Poor? A Synthesis of Findings from the Local-Level Institutions Study in Bolivia, Burkina Faso and Indonesia*. Washington DC: The World Bank.

Hall, J., ed. (1995) *Civil Society: Theory, History, Comparison*. Cambridge: Polity.

Hampshire, S. (1999) *Justice is Conflict*. Princeton: Princeton University Press.

Hann, C., and E. Dunn, eds. (1996) *Civil Society: Challenging Western Models*. London: Routledge.

Harbeson, J., D. Rothschild and N. Chazan, eds. (1994) *Civil Society and the State in Africa*. Boulder: Lynne Rienner.

Harris, F. (1999) 'Will the circle be unbroken? The erosion and transformation of African-American civic life', in R. Fullwinder (ed.), *Civil Society, Democracy and Civic Renewal*.

Harris, J. (2001) *Depoliticizing Development: The World Bank and Social Capital*. New Delhi: Lectword Books.

Hashemi, S. (1997) 'Building NGO legitimacy in Bangladesh', in D. Lewis (ed.), *International Perspectives on Voluntary Action*. London: Earthscan.

Heller, P. (1996) 'Social capital as a product of class mobilization and state intervention: industrial workers in Kerala, India', *World Development*, 24 (6), 1055–71.

Hirst, P. (1994) *Associative Democracy: New Forms of Economic and Social Governance*. Cambridge: Polity.

Howell, J., and J. Pearce. (2001) *Civil Society and Development: A Critical Exploration*. Boulder: Lynne Rienner.

Hulme, D., and M. Edwards, eds. (1997) *NGOs, States and Donors: Too Close for Comfort?* New York and London: Palgrave/Macmillan.

Ibrahim, S. (1995) 'Civil society and the prospects for democracy in the Arab world', in A. Norton (ed.), *Civil Society in the Middle East*. Leiden: E. J. Brill.

Jamal, A. (2003) 'Democratic citizens in non-democratic nations: civic participation and associational life in the West Bank', unpublished PhD thesis, Columbia University, New York.

Jenkins, R. (2002) 'Mistaking "governance" for "politics": foreign aid, democracy and the contribution of civil society', in S. Khilnani and S. Kaviraj (eds.), *Civil Society: History and Possibilities*.

Johnson, B. (2002) *Objective Hope: Assessing the Effectiveness of Faith-Based Organizations: a Review of the Literature*. University of Pennsylvania, Center for Research on Religion and Urban Civil Society.

Jordan, J. (1992) *Technical Difficulties: African-American Notes on the State of the Union*. New York: Pantheon.

Kaldor, M. (2003) *Global Civil Society*. Cambridge: Polity.

Keane, J., ed. (1988) *Civil Society and the State: New European Perspectives*. Cambridge: Polity.

Keane, J. (1998) *Civil Society: Old Images, New Visions*. Stanford: Stanford University Press.

Keane, J. (2001) Unpublished book proposal on the 'History of Democracy'.

Keane, J. (2003) *Global Civil Society*. Cambridge: Cambridge University Press.

Kelsay, J. (2002) 'Civil society and government in Islam', in R. Post and N. Rosenblum (eds.), *Civil Society and Government*.

Khalaf, S. (2002) *Civil and Uncivil Violence in Lebanon: A History of the Internationalization of Communal Conflict in Lebanon*. New York: Columbia University Press.

Khilnani, S. (2002) 'The development of civil society', in S. Khilnani and S. Kaviraj (eds), *Civil Society: History and Possibilities*.

Khilnani, S., and S. Kaviraj, eds. (2002) *Civil Society: History and Possibilities*. Cambridge: Cambridge University Press.

Klein, N. (2000) *No Logo: Taking Aim at the Brand Bullies*. London: Picador.

Klein, N. (2002) *Fences and Windows: Dispatches from the Front Lines of the Globalization Debate*. London: Picador.

Knight, B., and P. Stokes (1996) *The Deficit in Civil Society in the UK*. Birmingham: Foundation for Civil Society, Working Paper 1.

Konrad, G. (1989) *Anti Politics*. New York: Bookthrift.

Ladd, E. (1999) *The Ladd Report*. New York: The Free Press.

Lasch, C. (1996) *The Revolt of the Elites and the Betrayal of Democracy*. New York: W. W. Norton.

Lessig, L. (2001) *The Future of Ideas: The Fate of the Commons in a Connected World*. New York: Random House.

Levi, M. (1996) 'Social and unsocial capital: review of *Making Democracy Work*', *Politics and Society*, 24 (1), 45–55.

Levine, P. (2002) *Building the Electronic Commons*. University of Maryland, Democracy Collaborative.

Lewis, D. (2002) 'Civil society in African contexts: reflections on the usefulness of a concept', *Development and Change*, 33 (4), 569–86.

Li, X. (1999) 'Democracy and uncivil societies: a critique of civil society determinism', in R. Fullwinder (ed.), *Civil Society, Democracy and Civic Renewal*.

Lichtenstein, N. (2002) *State of the Union: A Century of American Labor*. Princeton: Princeton University Press.

Luther Adams, J. (1986) *Voluntary Associations*. Chicago: Exploration Press.

Majed, Z. (1998) 'Civil society in Lebanon.' *Kettering Review* (Fall), 36–43.

Mamdani, M. (1996) *Citizen and Subject: Contemporary Africa and the Legacy of Late Colonialism*. Princeton: Princeton University Press.

Mardin, S. (1995) 'Civil society and Islam', in J. Hall (ed.), *Civil Society: Theory, History, Comparison*.

Mathews, J. (1997) 'Power shift', *Foreign Affairs* (January/February), 50–66.

McClain, L., and J. Fleming, (2000) 'Some questions for civil society revivalists', *Chicago-Kent Law Review*, 75 (2), 301–54.

McConnell, C. (2003) 'Advanced democracy', *YES Magazine* (Winter), 41–2.

Mertes, T. (2002) 'Grassroots globalism: reply to Michael Hardt', *New Left Review*, 17 (September/October).

Metzger, T. (2002) 'The Western concept of civil society in the context of Chinese history', in S. Khilnani and S. Kaviraj (eds.), *Civil Society: History and Possibilities*.

Minkoff, D. (2002a) 'The emergence of hybrid organizational forms: combining identity-based service provision and political action', *Non Profit and Voluntary Sector Quarterly*, 31 (5), 377–401.

Minkoff, D. (2002b) 'Walking a political tightrope: responsiveness and internal accountability in social movement organizations', in E. Reid and M. Montilla (eds.), *Exploring Organizations and Advocacy: Governance and Accountability*. Washington DC: Urban Institute.

Myers, S. (1996) *Democracy is a Discussion: Civic Engagement in Old and New Democracies*. New London: Connecticut College.

Nosco, P. (2002) 'Confucian perspectives on civil society and government', in R. Post and N. Rosenblum (eds.), *Civil Society and Government*.

O'Connell, B. (1999) *Civil Society: The Underpinnings of American Democracy*. Hanover: University Press of New England.

Patel, S., J. Bolnick, and D. Mitlin (2001) 'Squatting on the global highway: community exchanges for urban transformation', in M. Edwards and J. Gaventa (eds.), *Global Citizen Action*.

Perez-Diaz, V. (1993) *The Return of Civil Society: The Emergence of Democratic Spain*. Cambridge: Harvard University Press.

Peters, P., and J. Scarpacci (1998) *Cuba's New Entrepreneurs: Five Years of Small-Scale Capitalism*. Arlington: Alexis de Tocqueville Institute.

Post, R., and N. Rosenblum (2002) 'Introduction', in R. Post and N. Rosenblum (eds.), *Civil Society and Government*. Princeton: Princeton University Press.

Pritchett, L., and D. Kaufman (1998) 'Civil liberties, democracy and the performance of government projects', *Finance and Development* (March), 26–9.

Putnam, R. (1993) *Making Democracy Work: Civic Traditions in Modern Italy*. Princeton: Princeton University Press.

Putnam, R. (2000) *Bowling Alone: The Collapse and Revival of American Community*. New York: Simon and Schuster.

Ray, M. (2002) *The Changing and Unchanging Face of US Civil Society*. New Brunswick: Transaction Publishers.

Reilly, C., ed. (1995) *New Paths to Democratic Development in Latin America: The Rise of NGO-Municipal Collaboration*. Boulder: Lynne Rienner.

Rieff, D. (1999) 'The false dawn of civil society', *The Nation* (22 February), 11–16.

Rifkin, J. (1995) *The End of Work: The Decline of the Global Labor Force and the Dawn of the Post-Market Era*. New York: G. P. Putnam.

Robin, C. (2001) Missing the point. A review of *Bowling Alone, Dissent* (Spring), 108–11.

Robinson, M., and G. White (1997) The role of civic organizations in the provision of social services', Conference on Public Sector Management for the Twenty-First Century, University of Manchester, 29 June–2 July.

Roepke, W. (1996) *The Moral Foundations of Civil Society*. New Brunswick: Transaction Publishers.

Rosen, J. (2001) *What are Journalists For?* New Haven: Yale University Press.

Rosenblum, N. (1998) *Membership and Morals: the Personal Uses of Pluralism in America*. Princeton: Princeton University Press.

Rosenblum, N. (1999) 'The moral uses of pluralism', in R. Fullwinder (ed.), *Civil Society, Democracy and Civic Renewal*.

Salamon, L. (1993) *The Global Associational Revolution: The Rise of the Third Sector on the World Scene*. Johns Hopkins University, Institute for Policy Studies, Occasional Paper 15.

Salamon, L., and H. Anheier (1997). 'The Third World's third sector in comparative perspective', in L. Salamon and H. Anheier (eds.), *The Nonprofit Sector in the Developing World*. Manchester: Manchester University Press.

Salamon, L., and H. Anheier (1999) 'Civil society in comparative perspective', in L. Salamon and H. Anheier (eds.), *Global Civil Society: Dimensions of the Non-Profit Sector*. Johns Hopkins University: Center for Civil Society Studies.

Salem, P. (1998) 'Deconstructing civil society: reflections on a paradigm.' *Kettering Review* (Fall), 8–15.

Sampson, S. (1996) 'The social life of projects: importing civil society to Albania', in C. Hann and E. Dunn (eds.), *Civil Society: Challenging Western Models*.

Scholte, J. (2002) *Democratizing the Global Economy: the Role of Civil Society*. Coventry: University of Warwick, Centre for the Study of Globalization.

Seligman, A. (1992) *The Idea of Civil Society*. Princeton: Princeton University Press.

Seligman, A. (2002) 'Civil society as idea and ideal', in S. Chambers and W. Kymlicka (eds.), *Alternative Conceptions of Civil Society*.

Singer, P. (2002) *One World: The Ethics of Globalization*. New Haven: Yale University Press.

Skocpol, T. (1999) 'Advocates without members: the recent transformation of American civic life', in T. Skocpol and M. Fiorina (eds.), *Civic Engagement in American Democracy*.

Skocpol, T. (2003) *Diminished Democracy: From Membership to Management in American Civic Life*. Oklahoma City: University of Oklahoma Press.

Skocpol, T., and M. Fiorina (1999) 'Making sense of the civic engagement debate', in T. Skocpol and M. Fiorina (eds.), *Civic Engagement in American Democracy*. Washington DC: Brookings Institution Press.

Smillie, I. (1996) *Service Delivery or Civil Society? NGOs in Bosnia and Hercegovina*. Ottawa: CARE Canada.

Tarrow, S. (1996) 'Making social science work across space and time: a critical reflection on Robert Putnam's Making Democracy Work', *American Political Science Review*, 90 (2), 389–97.

Tarrow, S. (1998) *Power in Movement: Social Movements and Contentious Politics*. Cambridge: Cambridge University Press.

Tendler, J. (1996) *Good Government in the Tropics*. Cambridge, Ma: MIT Press.

Uphoff, N. (1993) 'Grassroots organizations and NGOs in rural development: opportunities with diminishing states and expanding markets'. *World Development*, 21 (4), 607–22.

Uvin, P. (1998) *Aiding Violence: the Development Enterprise in Rwanda*. West Hartford: Kumarian Press.

Van Rooy, A., ed. (1998) *Civil Society and the Aid Industry*. London: Earthscan.

Van der Veer, P. (2002) 'Civic calm', *Biblio* (November/December), 34–5.

Varshney, A. (2002) *Ethnic Conflict and Civic Life: Hindus and Muslims in India*. New Haven: Yale University Press.

Verba, S., K. Schlozman and H. Brady (1995) *Voice and Equality: Civic Voluntarism in American Politics*. Cambridge, Ma: Harvard University Press.

Walzer, M. (1998) 'The idea of civil society: a path to social reconstruction', in E. J. Dionne (ed.), *Community Works*.

Warren, M. (2001) *Democracy and Association*. Princeton: Princeton University Press.

Warren, M. (2001) *Dry Bones Rattling: Community Building to Revitalize American Democracy*. Princeton: Princeton University Press.

Wasserman, D. (1999) 'Self-help groups, community and civil society', in R. Fullwinder (ed.), *Civil Society, Democracy and Civic Renewal.*

White, G. (1994) 'Civil society, democratization and development: clearing the analytical ground', *Democratization*, 1 (3).

White, J. (1996) 'Civic culture and Islam in urban Turkey', in C. Hann and E. Dunn (eds.), *Civil Society: Challenging Western Models.*

Wolfe, A. (1998) 'Is civil society obsolete?', in E. J. Dionne (ed.), *Community Works.*

Woolcock, M. (1998) 'Social capital and economic development: toward a theoretical synthesis and policy framework', *Theory and Society*, 27 (2), 151–208.

Wuthnow, R. (1999) 'Mobilizing civic engagement: the changing impact of religious involvement', in T. Skocpol and M. Fiorina (eds.), *Civic Engagement in American Democracy.*

Xiaoguang, K. (2002) *An Evaluation of the State of Development of Chinese NGOs and Suggestions for Capacity-Building.* Beijing: Chinese Academy of Sciences Research Centre.

Zadek, S. (2001) *The Civil Corporation.* London: Earthscan.

Zubaida, S. (2002) 'Civil society, community and democracy in the Middle East', in S. Khilnani and S. Kaviraj (eds.), *Civil Society: History and Possibilities.*

Index